Mediterranean Diet Cookbook UK

Quick, Easy & Incredibly Tasty Mediterranean Diet Recipes for Healthy Meals that the Whole Family Can Enjoy.

Author: Amelia Williams

TABLE OF CONTENTS

Hey there!

I would like to thank you for your trust and I really hope you'll enjoy the book.

A lot of thought and effort went into creating the book. I am not a part of a big publishing company and I take care of the whole publishing process myself in an effort to make sure your cooking journey is as smooth as possible.

If for any reason you did not like the book you can write on my email at deliciousrecipes.publishing@gmail.com. I always make sure to get back to everybody and if you're not happy with the book I can share another book.

I'm trying really hard to create the best cookbooks I can and I'm always open to constructive criticism.

Enjoy!

Everything You Need To Know About The Mediterranean Diet

If you have recently come across the Mediterranean diet, you might be wondering if this diet is for you, and what it involves. It's important to note that this is not a strict plan like some diets. It has no calorie counting or tracking of nutrients. Instead, it's a way of eating that focuses on whole grains, beans, olive oil, and lots of fresh fruit and vegetables. This sort of diet is a great way to lower your cholesterol and your risk of certain diseases, and we'll cover that in the following chapters.

This diet works on an "approved foods" list, which means that it is very flexible and it's easy to make it a part of your everyday life, rather than having to follow a set plan which dictates what you must eat even if you don't feel like it.

The main protein associated with the Mediterranean diet is fish, rather than pork or poultry or red meat. You may occasionally see poultry in Mediterranean recipes, but it's rare to see anything like red meat. Eggs are sometimes included, however.

The Mediterranean diet has enjoyed popularity in recent years because it has been noted that many people who live in the Mediterranean region (e.g. Italy, Spain, Greece) live long, healthy lives – and a lot of this has been attributed to the diets they follow.

While different food is of course associated with these different countries, there is a general trend toward the foods mentioned above, and some of the rules of thumb that you may wish to follow for this diet include:

- Plant-based oils, particularly olive oil, but also other more unusual oils. Avocado oil, for example, is popular, along with several of the nut butters. The emphasis is on high quality foods that bring out rich flavours.

- Eating dairy in moderation. You do not need to cut out dairy entirely to enjoy the Mediterranean diet, but you will likely find that you cut back on it considerably. Over time, your tastes will adjust to the reduction and this helps to keep the diet in line with its low cholesterol benefits.

- Eating less white sugar. White sugar does not have much of a place in Mediterranean main meals.

- Eating fewer animal products overall; while the diet does include some eggs, poultry, and fish, its focus is more on vegetables and fruits. You will still consume meat (if you wish to), but it will be accompanied by vegetables.

- Eating a lot of plants. This diet is based on vegetables and fruits, and you should be eating at least five portions of them in a day.

- Including some whole grains like brown rice and bulgur wheat. Few processed foods make their way into the Mediterranean diet, so white pasta and white rice are rarely to be found.

- Sensible consumption of red wine. Many people associate the Mediterranean diet with red wine, and if you are expecting to over-indulge, you will be disappointed. While red wine is drunk frequently, it is only consumed in moderation. Most women drink just a five ounce glass per day, while some men might drink two.

- Plenty of water every day. This may not sound like part of a diet to you, but keeping yourself hydrated is an important part of being healthy, and it is recognized in these hot countries in particular.

You might be wondering where to start. The answer is to start slowly, and not try to change all your meals at once. Begin with a meal a day, or even a meal every two to three days if you are finding it hard. Change your portion sizes, increasing the vegetables and decreasing or swapping out the meat.

Reduce your dependence on processed meats, high-fat dairy products, and flavoured, sweet yogurts. Once you've done this, you're well on the way to following a Mediterranean diet. Next, we're going to talk about how this kind of diet can help you lose weight and increase your metabolism, and then we'll move onto the other health benefits and how to cook Mediterranean meals.

How The Mediterranean Diet Helps You Improve Your Metabolism

The Mediterranean diet is not about fast weight loss or overnight results, but consistent adherence to the diet will help you to lose weight over time. Multiple studies, such as the Systematic Review of the Mediterranean Diet for Long-Term Weight Loss,[1] found that the Mediterranean diet resulted in greater weight loss than a comparable low-fat diet over a period of 12 months. That means if you're looking to revamp your eating in a way that helps you lose a few pounds sustainably and does not involve living on cottage cheese for life, a Mediterranean diet is probably perfect for you. It has the benefit of being highly flexible, and not requiring you to constantly track calories, cheat foods, or specific intakes of X, Y, or Z. This makes it easier to maintain than many of the stricter diets, meaning you are more likely to follow it sustainably. The diet's flexibility also means you can branch out and try new recipes when you're starting to get bored without having to do a whole host of calculations about whether new meals fit with your plan. You simply need to bring anything new you want to try into line with the general principles listed in the previous chapter, and you'll be fine. This means that if you fancy red meat one night, you can eat it, as long as you remember that in general, you should be minimizing it. If you need a sugar hit, that's fine too – just cut back at other times. The lack of hard rules makes this diet very sustainable and easy to incorporate into your lifestyle.

It's also thought that the Mediterranean diet may help to improve your metabolism. Less research has gone into this so far, but it is known that resistant starch (found in many of the foods eaten in the Mediterranean diet) helps to burn fat and might even reduce fat accumulation. This may have a metabolic effect, improving your metabolism in the long-term.

Far more study is needed to prove this conclusively, but it is worth considering if you are concerned about your metabolism and you would like to improve it. You can combine a Mediterranean diet with other techniques if necessary.So, sustained weight loss and the potential to improve your metabolism – these both make the Mediterranean diet seem like a win from all angles, but there are further health benefits, which we will cover in the following chapter.

---

1   Mancini JG, Filion KB, Atallah R, Eisenberg MJ. Systematic Review of the Mediterranean Diet for Long-Term Weight Loss. Am J Med. 2016 Apr;129(4):407-415.e4. doi: 10.1016/j.amjmed.2015.11.028. Epub 2015 Dec 22. PMID: 26721635.

Health Benefits Of The Mediterranean Diet

The Mediterranean diet is thought to help with many health problems, and a lot of people are migrating to this diet for the health benefits it offers.

Heart Disease & Stroke

Firstly, it is believed that this diet can reduce your risk of heart disease and strokes. Eating more healthy fats (such as olive oil) and plenty of nuts and avocados is good for your heart, and all of these things are in line with the Mediterranean diet.

Other parts of the diet that contribute to heart health include the consumption of whole grains (e.g. whole-wheat pasta and brown rice) and high-quality proteins such as fish and poultry. A further recommendation for good heart health is to limit your intake of refined breads, pastas, and processed meats. As these are all the fundamentals of a Mediterranean diet, so following the diet can really help improve your heart health.

It's also important to note that cutting down on processed meats and sugary foods will improve your heart, and these are foods that are generally excluded by this kind of diet. The same goes for salty foods, as the diet mostly depends on spices for flavouring. Given that most of us are looking for ways to reduce our sodium intake, this diet is an ideal solution.

Because it depends on lots of fresh vegetables, rather than tinned alternatives (which are often high in salt), the Mediterranean diet helps fight heart disease in many different ways.

Type 2 Diabetes

A study done by Mariette Gerber and Richard Hoffman (The Mediterranean diet: health, science and society)[2] also indicates that this diet can reduce your chance of developing type 2 diabetes. This may be partly due to the olive oil in the diet, but is also a result of the generally healthier lifestyle choices of people who follow this diet (such as spending a lot of time outdoors). It's thought that the whole Mediterranean lifestyle, rather than just the diet, could be beneficial to our health.

It is also possible that because the diet is rich in fibre, which the body digests slowly, it prevents swings in blood sugar. High levels of fibre can help to move fats through your bloodstream, reducing the amount that the body absorbs, and lowering "bad" cholesterol levels.

Fibre has the added benefit of helping you to feel full for longer, which may help you to eat

---

2   Gerber M, Hoffman R. The Mediterranean diet: health, science and society. Br J Nutr. 2015 Apr;113 Suppl 2:S4-10. doi: 10.1017/S0007114514003912. PMID: 26148921.

less overall. For many people, this results in lower cravings for sugar and sweetness, which is best for people who are borderline or have type 2 diabetes.

Cancer

It has been suggested by many studies that following a Mediterranean diet may help to reduce your chance of getting certain kinds of cancer. A review of 83 studies on this subject was done in 2017, called Adherence to Mediterranean Diet and Risk of Cancer: An Updated Systematic Review and Meta-Analysis.[3] It's thought to be particularly effective against cancers such as colorectal cancer and breast cancer. Again, it seems likely that the inclusion of extra-virgin olive oil is partially responsible for this health improvement.

It is important to note that for most of these health benefits, further study is needed to confirm them, but it seems to be generally accepted by the medical community that a Mediterranean diet can offer significant benefits to people's wellness and reduce their chances of suffering from certain diseases.

---

3   Schwingshackl L, Schwedhelm C, Galbete C, Hoffmann G. Adherence to Mediterranean Diet and Risk of Cancer: An Updated Systematic Review and Meta-Analysis. Nutrients. 2017 Sep 26;9(10):1063. doi: 10.3390/nu9101063. PMID: 28954418; PMCID: PMC5691680.

How Seniors Can Benefit From A Mediterranean Diet

If you are an older adult, you may have read the previous chapter with particular interest, as you are somewhat more likely to be at risk of these diseases than a young person. Heart disease, strokes, type 2 diabetes, and cancer are more likely to be of concern to you if you are over sixty-five.

However, there are further reasons you can benefit from a Mediterranean diet if you're getting on in years. There are many age-related problems that this diet may offer some protection against. With that in mind, let's explore the other ways in which this sort of food may help you out.

Agility

As an older adult, you may find that the balanced and nutritious diet helps to keep your muscles strong and reduces feelings of frailty. Increasing the number of fruits and vegetables that you consume will ensure that your body has what it needs to keep building muscles and retain its fitness levels.

Rheumatoid Arthritis

Many people start to suffer from rheumatoid arthritis as they grow older. An autoimmune disease where the body's immune system starts attacking the joints and makes them painful and swollen, this is a highly unpleasant and debilitating problem, and can take away the ability to do many of the things that you enjoy.

The Mediterranean diet is rich in anti-inflammatory omega-3 fatty acids, thanks to its reliance on fish as a main source of meat/protein. It is thought that these can help to inflammation and swelling, making you more comfortable and increasing the things you can do on a daily basis.

Neurodegenerative Diseases

Furthermore, this diet could help to reduce your risk of neurodegenerative diseases, including Parkinson's disease. Again, this is likely due to the inclusion of the unsaturated fatty acids that are gleaned from the fish and olive oil components, and the high levels of vitamin C, vitamin E, and flavonoids that are found in the diet's high quantities of fruits, vegetables, and wines.

Because the diet may also improve your cholesterol and your blood sugar levels, it can improve the health of your blood vessels. This is obviously beneficial in a great many ways, but it is thought that it may be able to reduce your risk of Alzheimer's disease and dementia.

Healthy Gut Biomes

The restricted diets which some elderly people must follow due to eating problems and other health issues can lead to reduced diversity in the microbial balance of the gut. We are becoming increasingly aware of the importance of good gut microbes, and poor diversity is thought to contribute to overall frailty, as well as impaired cognitive function.

Following a Mediterranean diet has been associated with improved gut microbiota; a study[4] done across several different European countries showed that following a Mediterranean diet for twelve months had a positive impact on the gut microbiota. This was then associated with reduced inflammation and frailty, as well as an improvement to cognitive function. By the end of the study, the subjects (who began with very diverse microbiota compositions) all showed similar gut microbiomes.

We don't yet fully understand how much of an impact an unhealthy gut has on the human body, but it has been connected with a plethora of health problems, including obesity.

Overall, if you are ageing, you may see even more benefits from following a Mediterranean diet than a young person – although both groups can improve their health by doing so.

---

4   Ghosh TS, Rampelli S, Jeffrey IB, et al, Mediterranean diet intervention alters the gut microbiome in older people reducing frailty and improving health status: the NU-AGE 1-year dietary intervention across five European countries. *BMJ Gut;* 2020: 69(7).

Top 5 Cooking Tips You Must Know When Cooking Mediterranean Meals

So, let's look at some of the top tips that will help you out if you are aiming to make your meals more Mediterranean.

Tip One: Use Oil and Greek Yogurt

When your cooking calls for butter or cream, switch them to oil or yogurt. You can do this very easily in most cases, and although it may take you a little while to adjust to the flavour, this is an excellent way to start enjoying the health benefits of the Mediterranean diet quickly and easily. For example, if making mashed potatoes, you do not need to add butter and cream to the pan when mashing. Instead, add a little olive oil and a spoonful of Greek yogurt.

You may already have noticed that olive oil is given prime place as one of the key ingredients that offers many of the health benefits already discussed (although researchers have stressed that it is not the only important element of the Mediterranean diet), so it makes sense to use this in place of butter where you can.

Using Greek yogurt in place of cream will also help you; it offers some of the same silky, creamy texture you will be used to, but it is not as fatty as cream.

Try this wherever you can see an opportunity to make swaps. You can even dip bread in olive oil instead of spreading it with salty, fatty butter. It will probably take a while to get used to the new flavours, but this is a great way to make your general diet adhere more closely to a Mediterranean one.

Tip Two: Implement Meat-Free Days

If you are a heavy meat-eater, you may find this hard at first, but it's important to try. You can add fish as an alternative to meat, or make some really tasty meals using vegetables and pulses and grains.

It may help if you meal plan, or specifically decide to go meat-free on a Monday. Planning in advance makes it easier to decide what you are going to have and get the ingredients ready, rather than suddenly realising you haven't thought about what to have for supper. You may also find it helps to cook entirely different meals, rather than omitting the meat from meals you already know and love. If you simply cut the meat out, you'll notice that it's gone and you're much more likely to miss it. If you make a different meal that you haven't had before, you can focus on the flavours and textures it offers without feeling that something has been taken away from you. If you are really missing meat, try to use poultry and fish substitutes, and limit your red meat days even if it is hard. You don't have to cut it out entirely, but cut down until you are happy with the quantity that you are consuming.

Tip Three: Focus on the Fruits and Vegetables

You will already have realised that the fruits and vegetables are the most important component in any Mediterranean meal. Rather than being seen as an accompaniment to meat, they are seen as the bulk of the food; meat is a side, an extra, and can be easily dispensed with if you prefer.

Remember that this goes for the grains too; they are an addition to the vegetables. They help you to feel full and they add texture and flavour, but they are not the main component of the meal. Plan your meals around the vegetables, and find ones that you really enjoy. Experiment with cooking them in different ways. Try roasting, frying, steaming, and boiling to create different textures and flavours. If you make vegetables more interesting and more important, you'll soon find you automatically focus on them.

Mediterranean food is very colourful, so make the most of the different vegetables to create visually appealing dishes that also taste amazing. Try to branch out and sample vegetables you haven't used before or rarely choose, and you'll find that your meals quickly shift to be balanced in the favour of the vegetables.

Tip Four: Add Salads

Instead of meat-based side dishes or piles of creamy mashed potatoes, try to include salads as the extra to your meals. Again, you can get very inventive here, using seasonally-available ingredients. It doesn't just have to be lettuce and tomatoes. Use nuts, dried fruit, cabbage, spinach, peppers, and anything else that takes your fancy, and create crispy, fresh salads to accompany any other meal you make. This is a great way to increase your intake of vegetables without feeling like you have to put too many in the main dish. It is also a nice way to enjoy fresh, raw vegetables.

This may particularly help if you are finding that you don't feel totally satisfied without the meat component of a dish, and it's also great for snacks if you are someone who gets hungry in between meals. You should also try including fruit salad as a dessert option instead of sugar-laden desserts. You are likely to find this odd at first, but if you are very used to having a sweet follow-up to a meal, this is a great way to meet that need without adding lots of refined sugar to your system.

Salads are bright, rich, and full of goodness, so use them wherever and however you can – winter or summer!

Tip Five: Keep It Simple

Mediterranean cooking does not need to be super complicated. You don't have to spend hours slaving in the kitchen to produce a meal that is gone in five minutes. You don't need to buy expensive, out-of-season ingredients and strange spices that you'll only use once. You can keep many of the meals that you are already familiar with, and just use substitutions to bring them into line with a Mediterranean diet.

You don't have to do anything very fancy to enjoy Mediterranean food. Many of their recipes are founded in simplicity, and focus on roasting or frying some of the vegetables you would eat anyway in olive oil.

You will probably find that the best way to stick to a Mediterranean diet is to experiment until you have found a handful of simple recipes that you enjoy and can adapt to suit the ingredients you generally have to hand (these may change as the seasons do). You can then use these recipes throughout the week, keeping a relatively small stock of ingredients and seasoning. You can always branch out and experiment more later, but start small or you risk getting overwhelmed.

Mediterranean cooking does not have to be complicated to be delicious and healthy.

Approved Food List

You may find it helpful to have a list of suggested foods to run through, along with a guide of how often you should be eating those things. Use this with some flexibility to help it fit with your habits and needs; it's here to serve as a starting point so you know what you should lean toward and what you should avoid.

Green Light Foods:
These are the foods you can eat in abundance, in almost any quantity that you want. Remember that balance is still important; nothing is good for you if you eat it to excess. Even vegetables can be bad if you exclusively dine on, for example, carrots!

However, these are the foods you should be depending upon for the bulk of your diet, and for the most part, you can consume them in large quantities.

Vegetables:

You can eat any vegetable that works for you, but here are some suggestions:

- Courgettes
- Peppers
- Potatoes
- Cabbage
- Kale
- Spinach
- Onions
- Garlic
- Avocados
- Brussels sprouts
- Beetroot
- Celery

Fruits:

Again, any fruit "goes" on a Mediterranean diet, but here are some ideas:

- Bananas
- Apples
- Berries
- Apricots
- Grapes
- Satsumas
- Dates

Legumes, Nuts, Seeds:

Most of these are also fitting for the Mediterranean diet, but here are some suggestions. Legumes and nuts will help you to feel full.

- Chickpeas
- Broad beans
- Kidney beans
- Lentils
- Almonds
- Walnuts
- Pine nuts
- Sunflower seeds
- Pumpkin seeds
- Sesame seeds

Whole Grains:

- Buckwheat
- Bulgur wheat
- Oats
- Quinoa
- Brown rice
- Wholegrain bread
- Whole-wheat pasta

Sea Food:

Small, oily fish are excellent for this diet and less damaging to the environment than taking the large fish from the sea. Where possible, try to choose small, tinned fish for minimal environmental impact.

- Sardines
- Mackerel
- Salmon
- Herring

Plant Oils:

- Extra virgin olive oil
- Rapeseed oil
- Avocado oil
- Flaxseed oil
- Almond oil

Herbs & Spices:

You can use any herbs and spices that you enjoy, but commonly used ones include:

- Parsley
- Mint
- Turmeric
- Coriander
- Cumin
- Basil

Amber Light Foods:

These are foods that you should try to moderate to a degree. It's a good idea to keep a rough tally of how much you are eating them, or only write them into your meal plan on occasion, in small quantities.

- Eggs
- Cheese (preferably unprocessed cheeses such as Brie, ricotta, and feta)
- Dairy products such as milk and cream
- Red wine
- Poultry
- Pork
- Lamb
- Beef
- Unflavoured yogurt

Red Light Foods:

These are the foods that you should try to avoid, or eat only rarely as a treat. You may find that it is better to allow yourself small amounts than to abstain entirely, but in general, these foods don't belong in a Mediterranean diet and should be limited.

- Refined carbohydrates, e.g. pastries, white bread, white rice
- Sweets/chocolate
- Sodas and other high-sugar beverages
- Red meat
- Fried foods, e.g. chips
- Processed meats like sausages

Use the Approved Foods list to guide you in making the right choices for your meals. Look for ways you can make substitutions to improve your diet, such as swapping processed meat for poultry, or exchanging chips for boiled potatoes. Test out different oils for different recipes, and see which ones work for you. It is important to find a balance in which the Mediterranean diet suits you and your needs, so that you can incorporate it as much as possible into your lifestyle.

Breakfast Recipes

Date Smoothie

Servings|2   Time|10 minutes

Nutritional Content (per serving):

Cal| 363   Fat| 1.7g   Protein| 17.9g   Carbs| 73.8g

Ingredients:

- ❖ 6 Medjool dates, pitted and chopped
- ❖ 30 grams almond butter
- ❖ 280 grams fat-free plain Greek yogurt
- ❖ 240 milliliters fresh apple juice
- ❖ 6-8 ice cubes

Directions:

1. In a high-speed blender, add all the ingredients and pulse until smooth and creamy.
2. Pour the smoothie into 2 serving glasses and serve immediately.

Fruity Smoothie

Servings|2   Time|10 minutes

Nutritional Content (per serving):

Cal| 217   Fat| 4.2g   Protein| 9.4g   Carbs| 39.5g

Ingredients:

- ❖ 1 banana, peeled and sliced
- ❖ 95 grams fresh strawberries
- ❖ 20 grams honey
- ❖ 360 milliliters unsweetened almond milk
- ❖ 125 grams frozen mango chunks
- ❖ 1¼ grams ground cinnamon
- ❖ 140 grams plain Greek yogurt
- ❖ 4-6 ice cubes

Directions:

1. In a high-speed blender, add all the ingredients and pulse until smooth and creamy.
2. Pour the smoothie into 2 serving glasses and serve immediately.

Oat Smoothie

Servings|2   Time|10 minutes

Nutritional Content (per serving):

Cal| 356   Fat| 14g   Protein| 9.7g   Carbs| 55.9g

Ingredients:

- 1½ frozen bananas, peeled and sliced
- 10 grams chia seeds
- 360 milliliters unsweetened almond milk
- 50 grams old-fashioned oats
- 30 grams peanut butter
- 30 grams honey
- 4-6 ice cubes

Directions:

1. In a high-speed blender, add all the ingredients and pulse until smooth and creamy.
2. Pour the smoothie into 2 serving glasses and serve immediately.

Avocado Toast

Servings|2   Time|18 minutes

Nutritional Content (per serving):

Cal| 415   Fat| 26g   Protein| 12.9g   Carbs| 37g

Ingredients:

- ❖ 1 large avocado, peeled, pitted and chopped roughly
- ❖ Salt and ground black pepper, as required
- ❖ 2 hard-boiled eggs, peeled and sliced
- ❖ 5 milliliters fresh lemon juice
- ❖ 5 grams fresh mint leaves, chopped finely
- ❖ 4 large rye bread slices

Directions:

1. In a bowl, add the avocado and with a fork, mash roughly.
2. Add the lemon juice, mint, salt and black pepper and stir to combine well. Set aside.
3. Heat a non-stick frying pan over medium-high heat and toast 2 slices for about 2 minutes per side.
4. Repeat with the remaining slices.
5. Spread the avocado mixture over each slice evenly.
6. Top with boiled eggs and serve immediately.

Ricotta Pear Toast

Servings|6   Time|15 minutes

Nutritional Content (per serving):

Cal| 218   Fat| 9.7g   Protein| 9.7g   Carbs| 24g

Ingredients:

For Ricotta Spread

- ❖ 250 grams part-skim whole milk ricotta cheese
- ❖ 50 grams almonds, sliced
- ❖ 10 grams orange zest, grated
- ❖ 10 grams honey
- ❖ 1¼ grams almond extract

For Serving

- ❖ 6 whole-grain bread slices, toasted
- ❖ 1 pear, cored and sliced
- ❖ 10 grams almonds, sliced
- ❖ 20 grams honey

Directions:

1. In a bowl, add the ricotta, almonds, almond extract and orange zest and gently stir to combine.
2. Drizzle with 5 grams of honey and mix well.
3. Spread ricotta spread onto each bread slice evenly and top each with pear slices, almonds and honey.

Figs Yogurt Bowl

Servings|4   Time|17 minutes

Nutritional Content (per serving):

Cal| 324   Fat| 5.9g   Protein| 17.6g   Carbs| 55.8g

Ingredients:

- ❖ 60 grams honey, divided
- ❖ 560 grams plain Greek yogurt
- ❖ 225 grams fresh figs, halved
- ❖ 30 grams pistachios, chopped

Directions:

1. In a medium wok, add half of the honey over medium heat and cook for about 1-2 minutes or until heated.
2. In the wok, place the figs, cut sides down and cook for about 5 minutes or until caramelized.
3. Remove from the heat and set aside for about 2-3 minutes.
4. Divide the yogurt into serving bowls and top each with the caramelized fig halves.
5. Sprinkle with pistachios.
6. Drizzle each bowl with the remaining honey and serve.

Overnight Oatmeal

Servings|1   Time|10 minutes

Nutritional Content (per serving):

Cal| 363   Fat| 7.5g   Protein| 10.1g   Carbs| 67.4g

Ingredients:

- ❖ 120 milliliters unsweetened almond milk
- ❖ 75 grams old-fashioned oats
- ❖ 20 grams maple syrup
- ❖ 30 grams fresh strawberries, hulled and sliced

Directions:

1. In a small bowl, add the milk and maple syrup and mix until well combined.
2. Place the oats into a 1-pint Mason jar and top with almond milk mixture.
3. Cover the jar and refrigerate overnight.
4. In the morning, top the oatmeal with strawberry slices and serve immediately.

Barley Porridge

Servings|4   Time|40 minutes

Nutritional Content (per serving):

Cal| 211   Fat| 2.4g   Protein| 5.3g   Carbs| 43.9g

Ingredients:

- ❖ 720 milliliters water
- ❖ Salt, as required
- ❖ 25 milliliters fresh orange juice
- ❖ 240 milliliters warm unsweetened almond milk
- ❖ 165 grams pearl barley
- ❖ 250 grams mixed berries
- ❖ 10 grams chia seeds
- ❖ 10 grams honey

Directions:

1. In a saucepan, add the water, barley and a pinch of salt over medium-high heat and bring to a boil.
2. Adjust the heat to low and simmer, covered for about 25-30 minutes or until all the liquid is absorbed, stirring occasionally.
3. Meanwhile, for berry compote: in another small pan, add the berries, orange juice, chia seeds, orange zest and honey over medium heat and cook for about 10 minutes, stirring occasionally.
4. Remove from the heat and set aside to cool slightly.
5. In 4 serving bowls, divide the barley and almond milk and stir to combine.
6. Top each bowl with berry compote and serve immediately.

Dried Fruit Quinoa

Servings|4   Time|25 minutes

Nutritional Content (per serving):

Cal| 407   Fat| 9.9g   Protein| 14.5g   Carbs| 70.2g

Ingredients:

- ❖ 190 grams uncooked quinoa, rinsed
- ❖ 8 dried apricots, cut into bite-sized pieces
- ❖ 25 grams walnuts, chopped
- ❖ 480 milliliters water
- ❖ 8 dried figs, cut into bite-sized pieces
- ❖ 5 grams ground cinnamon
- ❖ 480 milliliters milk

Directions:

1. In a large pan, add the quinoa and water over medium heat and bring to a boil.
2. Adjust the heat to low and simmer, covered for about 15 minutes or until all the liquid is absorbed, stirring occasionally.
3. Meanwhile, in a large bowl, add the apricots, figs, walnuts and cinnamon and mix well.
4. Remove the pan of quinoa from the heat and with a fork, fluff it.
5. Add the quinoa into the bowl of dried fruit mixture and toss to coat well.
6. Divide the quinoa mixture into 4 mason jars and top each with 120 milliliters of almond milk.
7. Cover the jars and refrigerate overnight before serving.

Baked Quinoa

Servings|6   Time|1½ hours

Nutritional Content (per serving):

Cal| 370   Fat| 6.1g   Protein| 7.5g   Carbs| 76.2g

Ingredients:

- 900 grams ripe bananas, peeled and mashed
- 10 milliliters vanilla extract
- 1½ grams salt
- 600 milliliters unsweetened almond milk
- 80 grams pure maple syrup
- 70 grams molasses
- 15 grams ground cinnamon
- 190 grams red quinoa, rinsed
- 25 grams slivered almonds

Directions:

1. In the bottom of a 2½-3-quart casserole dish, add the mashed bananas, maple syrup, molasses, vanilla extract, cinnamon and salt and mix until well combined.
2. Add the quinoa and almond milk and mix until well combined.
3. Cover the casserole dish and refrigerate overnight.
4. Preheat your oven to 180 degrees C.
5. Remove the casserole dish from the refrigerator and with a fork, beat the quinoa mixture well.
6. With a piece of foil, cover the casserole dish and bake for approximately 1-1¼ hours or until all the liquid is absorbed and the top of the quinoa is set.
7. Now, set the oven to broiler on high.
8. Remove the foil and sprinkle the top of the quinoa mixture with sliced almonds.
9. With a spatula, press the almonds into the quinoa mixture lightly.
10. Broil for about 2-4 minutes.
11. Remove from the oven and set aside to cool for about 10 minutes before serving.

Yogurt Waffles

Servings|6   Time|34 minutes

Nutritional Content (per serving):

Cal| 250   Fat| 4.4g   Protein| 11.1g   Carbs| 40.9g

Ingredients:

- 260 grams all-purpose flour
- 5 grams ground cinnamon
- 1¼ grams sea salt
- 360 milliliters whole milk
- 15 grams honey
- 14 grams baking powder
- 2 large eggs
- 150 grams plain Greek yogurt
- 5 milliliters vanilla extract

Directions:

1. In a bowl, mix together the flour, baking powder, cinnamon and salt.
2. In another large bowl, add the remaining ingredients and beat until well combined.
3. Add the flour mixture and mix until well combined and smooth.
4. Preheat the waffle iron and then grease it.
5. Place desired amount of the mixture into preheated waffle iron and cook for about 4 minutes or until golden brown.
6. Repeat with the remaining mixture.
7. Serve warm.

Oats Pancakes

Servings|6   Time|1 hour

Nutritional Content (per serving):

Cal| 212   Fat| 7.9g   Protein| 5.4g   Carbs| 31.2g

Ingredients:

- ❖ 150 grams rolled oats
- ❖ 1 ripe banana, peeled
- ❖ 30 milliliters olive oil
- ❖ 8 grams baking powder
- ❖ 2 eggs
- ❖ 80 grams maple syrup
- ❖ 5 milliliters vanilla extract
- ❖ 30 milliliters water

Directions:

1. In a high-speed blender, add all the ingredients and pulse until smooth.
2. Transfer the oatmeal mixture into a bowl.
3. Heat a greased non-stick wok over medium heat.
4. Place desired amount of the mixture and with a spatula, spread in an even circle.
5. Cook for about 3-4 minutes.
6. Flip and cook for about 2-3 minutes.
7. Repeat with the remaining mixture.

Oat Blueberry Muffins

Servings|6   Time|37 minutes

Nutritional Content (per serving):

Cal| 309   Fat| 9.8g   Protein| 9.5g   Carbs| 48.8g

Ingredients:

- 95 grams whole-wheat pastry flour
- 65 grams sugar
- 2 grams baking soda
- 1 egg, beaten lightly
- 240 milliliters low-fat buttermilk
- 100 grams fresh blueberries
- 75 grams walnuts, toasted and chopped roughly
- 100 grams oats
- 4 grams baking powder
- 1½ grams salt
- 190 grams natural applesauce
- 1¼ grams vanilla extract
- 40 grams dates, pitted and chopped
- 60 milliliters boiling water

Directions:

1. Preheat your oven to 190 degrees C. Grease a 12 cups muffin tin.
2. In a bowl, mix together the flour, oats, baking powder, baking soda and salt.
3. In another large bowl, add the egg, applesauce, buttermilk and vanilla extract and beat until well combined.
4. Add the flour mixture and mix until just combined.
5. Gently fold in the blueberries, dates and walnuts.
6. Add the water and gently stir to combine.
7. Set the mixture aside for about 10-15 minutes.
8. Place the mixture into the prepared muffin cups evenly.
9. Bake for approximately 20-22 minutes or until a toothpick inserted in the center comes out clean.
10. Remove from the oven and place the muffin tin onto a wire rack to cool for about 5 minutes.
11. Carefully invert the muffins onto the wire rack to cool completely before serving.

Veggie Omelet

Servings|4   Time|30 minutes

Nutritional Content (per serving):

Cal| 198   Fat| 14g   Protein| 13.4g   Carbs| 5.8g

Ingredients:

- ❖ 5 milliliters olive oil
- ❖ 15 grams canned artichoke hearts, rinsed, drained and chopped
- ❖ 1 Roma tomato, chopped
- ❖ Salt and ground black pepper, as required
- ❖ 180 grams fresh fennel bulbs, sliced thinly
- ❖ 45 grams olives, pitted and chopped
- ❖ 6 eggs
- ❖ 55 grams goat cheese, crumbled

Directions:

1. Preheat your oven to 160 degrees C.
2. In a large ovenproof wok, heat the oil over medium-high heat and sauté the fennel bulb for about 5 minutes.
3. Stir in the artichoke, olives and tomato and cook for about 3 minutes.
4. Meanwhile, in a bowl, add the eggs, salt and black pepper and beat until well combined.
5. Place the egg mixture over veggie mixture and stir to combine.
6. Cook for about 2 minutes.
7. Sprinkle with the goat cheese evenly and immediately transfer the wok into the oven.
8. Bake for approximately 5 minutes or until eggs are set completely.
9. Remove from the oven and carefully transfer the omelet onto a cutting board.
10. Cut into desired sized wedges and serve.

Shakshuka

Servings|4   Time|1 hour

Nutritional Content (per serving):

Cal| 215   Fat| 15.7g   Protein| 10.5g   Carbs| 9.1g

Ingredients:

- ❖ 30 grams butter
- ❖ 100 grams tomato, chopped finely
- ❖ 4 large eggs
- ❖ Salt and ground black pepper, as required
- ❖ 4 small yellow onions, sliced
- ❖ 1 garlic clove, minced
- ❖ 85 grams feta cheese, crumbled
- ❖ 5 grams fresh parsley, minced

Directions:

1. In a large cast-iron wok, melt the butter over medium-low heat and stir in the onions, spreading in an even layer.
2. Adjust the heat to low and cook for about 30 minutes, stirring after every 5-10 minutes.
3. Add the tomatoes and garlic and cook for about 2-3 minutes, stirring frequently.
4. With the spoon, spread the mixture in an even layer.
5. Carefully, crack the eggs over onion mixture and sprinkle with the feta cheese, salt, and black pepper.
6. Cover the wok tightly and cook for about 10-15 minutes or until desired doneness of the eggs.
7. Serve hot with the garnishing of the parsley.

Poultry Recipes

Spiced Whole Chicken

Servings|6   Time|1 hour 50 minutes

Nutritional Content (per serving):

Cal| 490   Fat| 20.3g   Protein| 70.8g   Carbs| 3.2g

Ingredients:

- 60 milliliters extra-virgin olive oil
- 10 grams fresh lemon zest, grated
- 5 grams paprika
- 5 grams ground cumin
- 1 (1360-gram) whole chicken, neck and giblets removed
- 3 garlic cloves, minced
- 10 grams dried oregano, crushed
- 5 grams cayenne pepper
- 1½ grams ground fennel seeds
- Salt and ground black pepper, as required

Directions:

1. In a large bowl, add all the ingredients except for the chicken and mix until well combined.
2. Add the chicken and coat with the mixture generously.
3. Refrigerate to marinate overnight, turning occasionally.
4. Preheat your oven to 220 degrees C.
5. Remove the chicken from the bowl and arrange into a roasting pan.
6. Coat the chicken with marinade.
7. With a kitchen string, tie the legs and tuck the wings back under the body.
8. Roast for about 10 minutes.
9. Now, reduce the temperature of the oven to 180 degrees C and roast for about 1½ hours.
10. Remove from the oven and place the chicken onto a cutting board for about 10 minutes before carving.
11. With a sharp knife, cut the chicken into desired sized pieces and serve.

Fig Glazed Chicken Breasts

Servings|4   Time|35 minutes

Nutritional Content (per serving):

Cal| 420   Fat| 18.7g   Protein| 45.2g   Carbs| 16.9g

Ingredients:

- ❖ 4 (150-gram) boneless, skinless chicken breast halves
- ❖ Salt and ground black pepper, as required
- ❖ 85 grams dried figs, chopped finely
- ❖ 60 milliliters balsamic vinegar
- ❖ 5 grams fresh thyme, chopped and divided
- ❖ 30 milliliters olive oil, divided
- ❖ 90 grams onion, chopped
- ❖ 120 milliliters chicken broth
- ❖ 10 milliliters low-sodium soy sauce

Directions:

1. Season the chicken breast halves with 1½ grams of thyme, salt and black pepper evenly.
2. In a large nonstick wok, heat 15 milliliters of the oil over medium-high heat and cook the chicken for about 6 minutes per side.
3. With a slotted spoon, transfer the chicken onto a plate and with a piece of foil, cover to keep warm.
4. In the same wok, heat the remaining oil over medium heat and sauté the onion for about 3 minutes.
5. Stir in the figs, broth, vinegar and soy sauce and simmer for about 3 minutes.
6. Stir in the remaining thyme and salt and remove from the heat.
7. Cut chicken breast halves into long slices diagonally.
8. Serve the chicken slices with the topping of fig sauce.

Lemony Chicken Breasts

Servings|4   Time|22 minutes

Nutritional Content (per serving):

Cal| 234   Fat| 13.9g   Protein| 24.9g   Carbs| 2.1g

Ingredients:

- ❖ 4 (115-gram) boneless, skinless chicken breast halves
- ❖ 45 milliliters olive oil
- ❖ 45 milliliters fresh lemon juice
- ❖ Salt and ground black pepper, as required
- ❖ 3 garlic cloves, chopped finely
- ❖ 10 grams fresh parsley, chopped
- ❖ 5 grams paprika
- ❖ 1½ grams dried oregano

Directions:

1. With a fork, pierce chicken breasts several times.
2. In a large bowl, add all the ingredients except the chicken breasts and mix until well combined.
3. Add the chicken breasts and coat with the marinade generously.
4. Refrigerate to marinate for about 2-3 hours.
5. Preheat the grill to medium-high heat. Grease the grill grate.
6. Remove the chicken from bowl and shake off excess marinade.
7. Place the chicken breasts onto the grill and cook for about 5-6 minutes per side.
8. Remove from the grill and transfer the chicken breasts onto the serving plate.
9. Serve hot.

Herbed Chicken Thighs

Servings|6   Time|23 minutes

Nutritional Content (per serving):

Cal| 267   Fat| 13.5g   Protein| 33.1g   Carbs| 2.3g

Ingredients:

- ❖ 30 milliliters olive oil, divided
- ❖ 5 grams lemon zest, grated
- ❖ 5 grams dried thyme
- ❖ Salt and ground black pepper, as required
- ❖ 15 milliliters fresh lemon juice
- ❖ 10 grams dried oregano
- ❖ 5 grams dried rosemary
- ❖ 680 grams chicken thighs, trimmed

Directions:

1. Preheat your oven to 215 degrees C.
2. In a large bowl, add 15 milliliters of the oil, lemon juice, lemon zest, dried herbs, salt and black pepper and mix well.
3. Add the chicken thighs and coat with the mixture generously.
4. Refrigerate to marinate for at least 20 minutes.
5. In an oven-proof wok, heat the remaining oil over medium-high heat and sear the chicken thighs for about 2-3 minutes.
6. Immediately, transfer the wok into the oven and bake for approximately 6-10 minutes.
7. Serve hot.

Braised Chicken Thighs

Servings|6   Time|1 hour 5 minutes

Nutritional Content (per serving):

Cal| 495   Fat| 22.2g   Protein| 67.9g   Carbs| 2.1g

Ingredients:

- ❖ 6 (225-gram) bone-in chicken thighs
- ❖ 30 milliliters olive oil
- ❖ 720 milliliters chicken broth
- ❖ 8 sprigs fresh dill
- ❖ 5 grams fresh dill, chopped
- ❖ Salt and ground black pepper, as required
- ❖ ½ of onion, sliced
- ❖ 1½ grams ground turmeric
- ❖ 30 milliliters fresh lemon juice

Directions:

1. Sprinkle the chicken thighs with salt and black pepper.
2. In a large nonstick wok, heat the olive oil over high heat.
3. Place the chicken thighs, skin side down and cook for about 3-4 minutes.
4. With a slotted spoon, transfer the thighs onto a plate.
5. In the same wok, add onion over medium heat and sauté for about 4-5 minutes.
6. Return the thighs in wok, skin side up with broth, turmeric, salt and black pepper.
7. Place the dill sprigs and over thighs and bring to a boil.
8. Adjust the heat to medium-low and simmer, covered for about 40-45 minutes, coating the thighs with cooking liquid.
9. Discard the thyme sprigs and stir in the lemon juice.
10. Serve hot with the topping of chopped dill.

Chicken Piccata

Servings|4   Time|25 minutes

Nutritional Content (per serving):

Cal| 262   Fat| 10.9g   Protein| 31.6g   Carbs| 9.3g

Ingredients:

- ❖ 35 grams all-purpose flour
- ❖ 1¼ grams red pepper flakes
- ❖ 4 (115-gram) boneless chicken cutlets
- ❖ 1 shallot, chopped finely
- ❖ 2 garlic cloves, minced
- ❖ 240 milliliters chicken broth
- ❖ 30 grams Parmesan cheese, grated
- ❖ Salt and ground black pepper, as required
- ❖ 35 grams butter, divided
- ❖ 30 grams capers, drained
- ❖ 60 milliliters fresh lemon juice

Directions:

1. In a large shallow bowl, add the almond flour, Parmesan Cheese, red pepper flakes, salt and black pepper and mix well.
2. Coat the chicken with the flour mixture evenly.
3. In a wok, melt half of the butter over medium heat and cook the chicken pieces for about 3-5 minutes per side.
4. With a slotted spoon, transfer the chicken pieces onto a plate and cover with a piece of foil to keep warm.
5. In the same wok, melt the remaining butter over medium heat and sauté the shallot and garlic for about 3 minutes.
6. Stir in the capers, broth and lemon juice and cook for about 5 minutes.
7. Remove from the heat and pour over the chicken breasts.
8. Serve immediately.

Chicken Marsala

Servings|4   Time|45 minutes

Nutritional Content (per serving):

Cal| 535   Fat| 33.1g   Protein| 32.6g   Carbs| 19.4g

Ingredients:

- ❖ 65 grams all-purpose flour
- ❖ Salt and ground black pepper, as required
- ❖ 30 milliliters olive oil
- ❖ 225 grams fresh Cremini mushrooms, sliced
- ❖ 180 milliliters dry Marsala wine
- ❖ 5 grams fresh parsley, chopped

- ❖ 5 grams garlic powder
- ❖ 4 (115-gram) boneless, skinless chicken breasts
- ❖ 35 grams butter, divided
- ❖ 4 garlic cloves, minced
- ❖ 300 milliliters chicken broth
- ❖ 180 grams heavy cream

Directions:

1. In a shallow bowl, mix together the flour, garlic powder, salt and black pepper.
2. Coat the chicken breasts with the flour mixture evenly and then shake off excess.
3. In a 12-inch wok, heat oil and 30 grams of butter over medium-high heat and cook the chicken breasts in 2 for about 3-4 minutes per side.
4. With a slotted spoon, transfer the chicken breasts onto a warm plate and cover with a piece of foil to keep warm.
5. In the same wok, melt the remaining butter and cook the mushrooms for about 2-3 minutes, stirring frequently.
6. Add the garlic and cook for about 1 minute, stirring continuously.
7. Stir in the Marsala and the broth and simmer for about 10-15 minutes.
8. Stir in the chicken and cream and cook for about 3 minutes.
9. Serve immediately with the garnishing of parsley.

Bruschetta Chicken

Servings|4   Time|27 minutes

Nutritional Content (per serving):

Cal| 390   Fat| 23g   Protein| 39.2g   Carbs| 6.9g

Ingredients:

- 4 (115-gram) boneless, skinless chicken breasts
- Salt, as required
- 4 tomatoes, chopped finely
- 15 grams fresh basil, shredded
- 30 milliliters olive oil
- 5 grams garlic, minced
- 15 grams Italian seasoning
- 15 grams butter
- 3 garlic cloves, chopped
- 55 grams Parmesan cheese, shredded

Directions:

1. In a bowl, add the chicken, minced garlic, Italian seasoning and salt and mix well.
2. In a cast iron wok, melt the butter over medium-high heat and sear the chicken breasts for about 6 minutes per side or until done completely.
3. Meanwhile, for topping: in a bowl, add remaining ingredients except for the Parmesan cheese and mix.
4. Remove the wok from the heat and divide the chicken breasts onto serving plates.
5. Serve immediately with the topping of tomato mixture and Parmesan cheese.

Chicken Cacciatore

Servings|4   Time|1½ hours

Nutritional Content (per serving):

Cal| 489   Fat| 20.2g   Protein| 50.1g   Carbs| 23.9g

Ingredients:

- ❖ 45 milliliters olive oil, divided
- ❖ Salt and ground black pepper, as required
- ❖ 6 grams garlic, minced
- ❖ 2 small red capsicums, seeded and chopped
- ❖ 15 grams fresh basil, chopped
- ❖ 90 grams black olives, pitted
- ❖ 30 grams tomato paste
- ❖ 6 (150-gram) bone-in, skinless chicken thighs
- ❖ 1 medium onion, chopped
- ❖ 1 large carrot, peeled and sliced
- ❖ 285 grams fresh mushrooms, sliced
- ❖ 5 grams dried oregano
- ❖ 120 milliliters red wine
- ❖ 2½ (395-gram) cans crushed tomatoes

Directions:

1. Season the chicken thighs with salt and black pepper evenly.
2. In a heavy cast-iron wok, heat 30 milliliters of oil over medium-high heat and sear the chicken thighs for about 3-4 minutes per side.
3. With a slotted spoon, transfer the chicken thighs onto a plate.
4. In the same wok, heat the remaining oil over medium heat and sauté the onion and garlic for about 4-5 minutes.
5. Add the carrot, capsicums, mushrooms and herbs and cook for about 5 minutes.
6. Add the wine and cook for about 2-3 minutes.
7. Add the tomatoes, tomato paste, salt and black pepper and stir to combine.
8. Add the chicken thighs and stir to combine.
9. Reduce heat to low and simmer, covered for about 40 minutes, stirring occasionally.
10. Stir in the olives and simmer for about 10 minutes.
11. Serve immediately.

Chicken Parmigiana

Servings|4   Time|36 minutes

Nutritional Content (per serving):

Cal| 490 Fat| 26.3g   Protein| 42.7g   Carbs| 21.5g

Ingredients:

- 1 large egg, beaten
- 30 grams Parmesan cheese, grated
- 1½ grams paprika
- Salt and ground black pepper, as required
- 115 grams mozzarella cheese, sliced thinly
- 65 grams all-purpose flour
- 1½ grams dried parsley
- 1½ grams garlic powder
- 4 (150-gram) skinless, boneless chicken breasts
- 60 milliliters olive oil
- 450 grams marinara sauce

Directions:

1. Preheat your oven to 190 degrees C.
2. In a shallow dish, place the beaten egg.
3. In another shallow dish, place the almond flour, Parmesan, parsley, spices, salt, and black pepper and mix well.
4. Dip each chicken breast into the beaten egg and then coat with the flour mixture.
5. In a deep wok, heat the oil over medium-high heat and fry the chicken breasts for about 3 minutes per side.
6. With a slotted spoon, transfer the chicken breasts onto a paper towel-lined plate to drain.
7. In the bottom of a casserole dish, place about 150 grams of marinara sauce and spread evenly.
8. Arrange the chicken breasts over marinara sauce in a single layer.
9. Top with the remaining marinara sauce, followed by mozzarella cheese slices.
10. Bake for approximately 20 minutes or until done completely.
11. Remove from the oven and serve hot with the garnishing of fresh parsley.

Chicken & Olives Casserole

Servings|4   Time|35 minutes

Nutritional Content (per serving):

Cal| 332   Fat| 17.7g   Protein| 36.6g   Carbs| 5.7g

Ingredients:

- 1½ grams dried basil
- 2 (225-gram) chicken breasts, cut in half lengthwise
- 2 garlic cloves, minced
- 15 milliliters fresh lemon juice
- 90 grams black olives, chopped finely
- Salt and ground black pepper, as required
- 15 milliliters olive oil
- 240 milliliters chicken broth
- 150 grams cherry tomatoes, quartered
- 60 grams onion, chopped finely
- 55 grams feta cheese, crumbled

Directions:

1. Preheat your oven to 190 degrees C.
2. In a bowl, add the dried herbs, salt and black pepper and mix well.
3. Season the chicken with the herb mixture evenly.
4. In a cast iron wok, heat the oil over medium-high heat and cook the chicken for about 3 minutes per side.
5. With a slotted spoon, transfer the chicken breasts onto a plate.
6. In the same wok, add the garlic, broth and lemon juice over medium heat and cook for about 5 minutes.
7. Remove from the heat and stir in the cooked chicken breasts.
8. Spread the olives, tomatoes and onions on top of the chicken mixture evenly.
9. Bake for approximately 8 minutes.
10. Sprinkle with cheese and bake for approximately 3-4 minutes.
11. Remove from the oven and set aside for about 5-10 minutes before serving.

Chicken Risotto

Servings|3   Time|33 minutes

Nutritional Content (per serving):

Cal| 400   Fat| 18.5g   Protein| 43g   Carbs| 16.7g

Ingredients:

- 1 (150-gram) chicken breast, chopped
- 30 milliliters olive oil, divided
- 30 grams butter
- 180 grams Arborio rice
- 15 grams Parmesan cheese, grated
- Salt and ground black pepper, as required
- 5 milliliters fresh lemon juice
- 1 onion, chopped
- 960 milliliters chicken broth
- 70 grams frozen green peas

Directions:

1. Season the chicken pieces with salt and black pepper.
2. In a small skillet, heat 15 milliliters of oil over medium heat and cook the chicken pieces for about 5-7 minutes.
3. Remove from the heat and stir in the fresh lemon juice.
4. Transfer the chicken pieces onto a plate and with a piece of foil, cover to keep warm. Set aside.
5. In a pan, heat the remaining oil and butter over medium heat and sauté the onion for about 4-5 minutes.
6. Add the rice and cook for about 1 minute, stirring continuously.
7. Add one ladle of broth and cook until the liquid is absorbed, stirring continuously.
8. Repeat this process until all the broth is absorbed. (This process will take about 15-20 minutes).
9. Meanwhile, in another pan of water, boil the peas for about 10-15 minutes.
10. Drain the water and set aside.
11. In the pan of rice, stir in the chicken, peas, Parmesan, salt and black pepper and remove from the heat.
12. Serve immediately.

Chicken & Veggie Kabobs

Servings|8   Time|30 minutes

Nutritional Content (per serving):

Cal| 241   Fat| 11.5g   Protein| 27.7g   Carbs| 7.5g

Ingredients:

- ❖ 60 milliliters white vinegar
- ❖ 60 milliliters olive oil
- ❖ 5 grams dried thyme, crushed
- ❖ 910 grams skinless, boneless chicken breast, cubed into ½-inch size
- ❖ 1 courgette, sliced
- ❖ 1 large onion, quartered and separated into pieces
- ❖ 60 milliliters fresh lemon juice
- ❖ 2 garlic cloves, minced
- ❖ Salt and ground black pepper, as required
- ❖ 2 medium capsicums, seeded and cubed into 1-inch size
- ❖ 16 cherry tomatoes
- ❖ 16 fresh mushrooms, sliced

Directions:

1. In a large bowl, add the vinegar, fresh lemon juice, oil, garlic, thyme, salt, and black pepper and mix until well combined.
2. Add the chicken cubes and coat with mixture generously.
3. Refrigerate, covered to marinate for about 2-4 hours.
4. Preheat the outdoor grill to medium-high heat. Grease the grill grate.
5. Thread the chicken and vegetables onto pre-soaked wooden skewers, respectively.
6. Grill for about 10 minutes, flipping occasionally.
7. Serve hot.

Turkey & Rice Wok

Servings|6   Time|1½ hours

Nutritional Content (per serving)

Cal| 155   Fat| 4.7g   Protein| 12.1g   Carbs| 16.3g

Ingredients:

- 360 milliliters plus 90 milliliters water, divided
- 85 grams capsicum, seeded and chopped
- 5 grams Cajun seasoning
- 1½ grams garlic powder
- 1¼ grams ground black pepper
- 110 grams uncooked brown rice
- 225 grams ground turkey
- 45 grams onion, chopped
- 1½ grams garlic, minced
- 1½ grams dried celery flakes
- Salt, as required

Directions:

1. In a saucepan, add 360 milliliters of water and bring to a boil.
2. Add the rice and stir to combine.
3. Adjust the heat to low and simmer, covered for about 40-50 minutes or until all the liquid is absorbed.
4. Remove from the heat and set aside.
5. Heat a wok over medium heat and cook the ground turkey for about 2-3 minutes, stirring frequently.
6. Stir in the capsicum, onion and garlic and cook for about 5-8 minutes, stirring frequently.
7. Drain excess fat from the wok.
8. Stir in the cooked rice, spices and remaining water and bring to a gentle simmer.
9. Cook for about 10 minutes or until all the liquid is absorbed.
10. Serve hot.

Turkey Meatloaf

Servings|4   Time|58 minutes

Nutritional Content (per serving):

Cal| 354   Fat| 14.8g   Protein| 26.5g   Carbs| 6.4g

Ingredients:

- ❖ 10 milliliters olive oil
- ❖ 5 grams garlic, minced
- ❖ 40 grams feta cheese, crumbled
- ❖ 100 grams roasted capsicums, chopped
- ❖ 5 grams fresh parsley, chopped
- ❖ Salt and ground black pepper, as required
- ❖ 60 grams red onion, chopped
- ❖ 455 grams ground turkey
- ❖ 30 grams panko breadcrumbs
- ❖ 45 grams green olives, pitted and chopped
- ❖ 5 grams fresh dill, chopped
- ❖ 10 grams dried oregano
- ❖ 1 egg
- ❖ 15 milliliters milk

Directions:

1. Preheat your oven to 200 degrees C. Line a baking sheet with parchment paper.
2. In a non-stick wok, heat the oil over medium heat and sauté the onion and garlic for about 2-3 minutes.
3. Remove from the heat and transfer the mixture into a large mixing bowl.
4. In the bowl, add the remaining ingredients and mix until well combined.
5. Place the mixture onto the prepared baking sheet and shape into a loaf.
6. Bake for approximately 30-40 minutes.
7. Remove from the oven and set aside for about 10 minutes before serving.
8. Cut the meatloaf into desired sized slices and serve.

Red Meat Recipes

Pesto Steak

Servings|3   Time|37 minutes

Nutritional Content (per serving):

Cal| 472   Fat| 30.6g   Protein| 45.2g   Carbs| 5.8g

Ingredients:

- ❖ 10 grams fresh oregano, chopped
- ❖ 5 g lemon peel, grated
- ❖ Salt and ground black pepper, as required
- ❖ 125 grams pesto
- ❖ 5 grams garlic, minced
- ❖ 1½ grams red pepper flakes
- ❖ 455 grams boneless beef top sirloin steak

Directions:

1. Preheat the gas grill to medium heat. Lightly grease the grill grate.
2. In a bowl, add the oregano, garlic, lemon peel, red pepper flakes, salt and black pepper and mix well.
3. Rub the steak with garlic mixture evenly.
4. Place the steak onto the grill and cook, covered for about 12-17 minutes, flipping occasionally.
5. Remove from the grill and place the steak onto a cutting board for about 5 minutes.
6. With a sharp knife, cut the steak into desired sized slices.
7. Divide the steak slices onto serving plates and serve with the topping of pesto.

Stuffed Steak

Servings|6   Time|50 minutes

Nutritional Content (per serving):

Cal| 392   Fat| 20.5g   Protein| 47.4g   Carbs| 2g

Ingredients:

- ❖ 5 grams dried oregano
- ❖ 90 milliliters fresh lemon juice
- ❖ 1 (910-gram) beef flank steak, pounded into ½-inch thickness
- ❖ 30 grams frozen chopped spinach, thawed and squeezed
- ❖ 5 grams dried thyme
- ❖ 30 milliliters olive oil
- ❖ 100 grams olive tapenade
- ❖ 30 grams feta cheese, crumbled
- ❖ Salt, as required

Directions:

1. In a large baking dish, add the oregano, lemon juice and oil and mix well.
2. Add the steak and coat with the marinade generously
3. Refrigerate to marinate for about 4 hours, flipping occasionally.
4. Preheat your oven to 220 degrees C. Line a shallow baking dish with parchment paper.
5. Remove the steak from baking dish and place onto a cutting board.
6. Place the tapenade onto the steak evenly and top with the spinach, followed by the feta cheese.
7. Carefully roll the steak tightly to form a log.
8. With 6 kitchen string pieces, tie the log at 6 places.
9. Carefully cut the log between strings into 6 equal pieces, leaving the string in place.
10. Arrange the log pieces onto the prepared baking dish, cut-side up.
11. Bake for approximately 25-35 minutes.
12. Remove from the oven and set aside for about 5 minutes before serving.

Steak with Cheese Sauce

Servings|6   Time|1¼ hours

Nutritional Content (per serving):

Cal| 844   Fat| 69.7g   Protein| 37.6g   Carbs| 1.4g

Ingredients:

- ❖ 1000 grams heavy cream
- ❖ 85 grams Gorgonzola cheese, crumbled
- ❖ 1¼ grams onion powder
- ❖ 1¼ grams garlic powder
- ❖ 4 (225-gram) beef tenderloin steaks
- ❖ 25 grams Parmesan cheese, shredded
- ❖ Salt and ground black pepper, as required
- ❖ Pinch of lemon pepper seasoning

Directions:

1. In a pan, add the heavy cream over medium heat and bring to a boil.
2. Adjust the heat to low and simmer for about 1 hour, stirring occasionally.
3. Remove from the heat and immediately stir in both cheeses, salt and black pepper until well combined.
4. Meanwhile, in a small bowl, mix together the onion powder, garlic powder, lemon pepper, salt and black pepper.
5. Season the steaks with seasoning mixture evenly.
6. Preheat the outdoor grill to medium-high heat. Grease the grill grate.
7. Place the steaks onto the grill and cook for about 4-5 minutes per side.
8. Remove the steaks from the grill and place onto a cutting board for about 5-10 minutes.
9. Cut each steak into desired sized slices and transfer onto serving plates evenly.
10. Top with the creamy sauce and serve hot.

Braised Beef

Servings|8   Time|2¼ hours

Nutritional Content (per serving):

Cal| 462   Fat| 18.1g   Protein| 54.2g   Carbs| 13.5g

Ingredients:

- ❖ 60 milliliters vegetable oil
- ❖ 675 grams celery stalks, chopped
- ❖ 2 onions, chopped
- ❖ 4 garlic cloves, minced
- ❖ 240 milliliters dry red wine
- ❖ 15 grams fresh parsley, chopped
- ❖ Salt and ground black pepper, as required
- ❖ 1360 grams boneless beef chuck roast, cut into 1½-inch cubes
- ❖ 2 (680-gram) cans Italian-style stewed tomatoes
- ❖ 5 grams dried oregano

Directions:

1. In a saucepan, heat the oil over medium-high heat and sear the beef cubes for about 4-5 minutes.
2. Add the celery, onions and garlic and cook for about 5 minutes, stirring frequently.
3. Stir in the remaining ingredients and bring to a boil.
4. Reduce heat to low and simmer, covered for about 1½-1¾ hours or until desired doneness of beef.
5. Serve hot.

Beef & Veggie Bake

Servings|6   Time|2½ hours

Nutritional Content (per serving):

Cal| 344   Fat| 14.3g   Protein| 30.2g   Carbs| 18.6g

Ingredients:

- ❖ 30 milliliters olive oil
- ❖ 2 red onions, cut into thick wedges
- ❖ 500 grams plum tomatoes, quartered
- ❖ 140 grams canned green olives, drained
- ❖ 2 heads garlic, halved
- ❖ Salt and ground black pepper, as required
- ❖ 740 grams stewing steak, cut into large chunks
- ❖ 3 capsicums, seeded and cut into thick slices
- ❖ 30 grams sun-dried tomato paste
- ❖ 10 grams fresh oregano, chopped
- ❖ 240 milliliters red wine
- ❖ 240 milliliters water

Directions:

1. Preheat your oven to 190 degrees C.
2. In a roasting pan, heat the oil over medium heat and sear the steak chunks in 2 batches for about 5 minutes or until browned.
3. With a slotted spoon, transfer the steak chunks into a bowl.
4. In the same roasting pan, add the onions and capsicums and sauté for about 5 minutes.
5. Add the cooked steak chunks and remaining ingredients and stir to combine.
6. With a piece of the foil, cover the roasting tin and bake for approximately 1 hour.
7. Remove the foil and bake for approximately 1 hour more.
8. Serve hot.

Rosemary Pork Chops

Servings|4 Time|45 minutes

Nutritional Content (per serving):

Cal| 231 Fat| 10.9g Protein| 27.9g Carbs| 3.3g

Ingredients:

- ❖ 3 garlic cloves, minced
- ❖ Salt and ground black pepper, as required
- ❖ 5 grams fresh rosemary, minced
- ❖ 4 (150-gram) boneless pork loin chops

Directions:

1. Preheat your oven to 220 degrees C. Arrange a rack into a foil-lined shallow roasting pan.
2. In a bowl, add the garlic, rosemary, salt and black pepper and mix well.
3. Coat the chops with the rosemary mixture evenly.
4. Arrange the chops onto the rack in roasting pan.
5. Roast for about 10 minutes.
6. Now, set the temperature of oven to 180 degrees C and roast for about 25 minutes more.
7. Serve hot.

Pork Chops with Peach Glaze

Servings|4   Time|38 minutes

Nutritional Content (per serving):

Cal| 469   Fat| 27.6g   Protein| 37.7g   Carbs| 15.9g

Ingredients:

- ❖ 4 bone-in pork loin chops
- ❖ 30 milliliters extra-virgin olive oil
- ❖ 120 milliliters balsamic vinegar
- ❖ 5 grams fresh oregano, chopped
- ❖ 150 grams feta cheese, crumbled
- ❖ Salt and ground black pepper, as required
- ❖ 20 grams honey
- ❖ 2 peaches, pitted and sliced
- ❖ 15 grams fresh basil, chopped

Directions:

1. Preheat the broiler of the oven to high.
2. Season the pork chops with salt and black pepper evenly.
3. In a large ovenproof wok, heat the oil over medium-high heat and sear the pork chops for about 3-4 minutes per side.
4. Adjust the heat to medium and cook for about 6-8 minutes.
5. In a small bowl, add the balsamic vinegar, honey and oregano and beat until well combined.
6. Stir in the vinegar mixture and cook for about 2 minutes.
7. Remove from the heat and stir in the peaches.
8. Transfer the wok to the oven and broil for about 4-5 minutes or until the peaches are lightly charred.
9. Serve hot with the topping of feta and basil.

Pork Tenderloin

Servings|3   Time|32 minutes

Nutritional Content (per serving):

Cal| 321   Fat| 13.7g   Protein| 42.4g   Carbs| 5.2g

Ingredients:

- ❖ 5 grams fresh rosemary, minced
- ❖ 15 milliliters balsamic vinegar
- ❖ 5 milliliters fresh lemon juice
- ❖ 10 grams sugar
- ❖ Salt and ground black pepper, as required

- ❖ 1 garlic clove, minced
- ❖ 15 milliliters olive oil
- ❖ 5 grams Dijon mustard
- ❖ 455 grams pork tenderloin
- ❖ 35 grams blue cheese, crumbled

Directions:

1. Preheat your oven to 200 degrees C. Grease a large rimmed baking sheet.
2. In a large bowl, add all the ingredients except the pork tenderloin and cheese and beat until well combined.
3. Add the pork tenderloin and coat with the mixture generously.
4. Arrange the pork tenderloin onto the prepared baking sheet.
5. Bake for approximately 20-22 minutes.
6. Remove from the oven and place the pork tenderloin onto a cutting board for about 5 minutes.
7. With a sharp knife, cut the pork tenderloin into ¾-inch thick slices and serve with the topping of cheese.

Pork Chops with Mushroom Sauce

Servings|4   Time|31 minutes

Nutritional Content (per serving):

Cal| 417   Fat| 24.6g   Protein| 41.8g   Carbs| 6.7g

Ingredients:

- ❖ 4 boneless pork chops
- ❖ Salt and ground black pepper, as required
- ❖ 40 grams butter, divided
- ❖ ½ of medium onion, chopped finely
- ❖ 360 milliliters chicken broth
- ❖ 1½ grams paprika
- ❖ 10 milliliters olive oil
- ❖ 225 grams fresh mushrooms, sliced
- ❖ 2 garlic cloves, minced
- ❖ 10 grams flour
- ❖ 90 grams heavy whipping cream

Directions:

1. Season the pork chops with paprika, salt and black pepper evenly.
2. In a pan, heat oil and half of butter over medium-high heat and sear the chops for about 3-4 minutes per side.
3. With a slotted spoon, transfer the chops onto a plate.
4. In the same pan, melt half of the butter over medium heat and cook the mushrooms for about 2 minutes, stirring frequently.
5. Stir in the remaining butter, onions, salt and black pepper and cook for about 3-4 minutes, stirring frequently.
6. Add the garlic and cook for about 1 minute, stirring frequently.
7. Add the flour and stir vigorously for at least 30 seconds.
8. Add the broth, whipping cream, salt and black pepper and simmer for about 2 minutes, stirring continuously
9. Add in the pork chops and simmer, covered over low heat for about 5-8 minutes.
10. Serve hot.

Sausage with Capsicums

Servings|6   Time|27 minutes

Nutritional Content (per serving):

Cal| 415   Fat| 33.8g   Protein| 22.9g   Carbs| 4.8g

Ingredients:

- ❖ 15 milliliters olive oil
- ❖ 5 grams garlic powder
- ❖ Salt and ground black pepper, as required
- ❖ 8 pork sausages, sliced
- ❖ 4 small capsicums, seeded and sliced thinly

Directions:

1. In a large wok, heat the oil over medium-high heat and cook sausage for about 8-10 minutes.
2. With a slotted spoon, transfer the sausage slices into a large bowl and set aside.
3. In the same wok, add the capsicums and garlic powder and sauté for about 3-5 minutes.
4. Stir in the sausage, salt and black pepper and cook for about 1-2 minutes.
5. Serve hot.

Spiced Lamb Chops

Servings|8   Time|26minutes

Nutritional Content (per serving):

Cal| 385   Fat| 19.g   Protein| 47.9g   Carbs| 1.2g

Ingredients:

- ❖ 5 grams fresh mint, chopped
- ❖ 5 grams ground allspice
- ❖ Salt and ground black pepper, as required
- ❖ 2 racks of lamb, trimmed and separated into 16 chops
- ❖ 5 grams garlic paste
- ❖ 5 grams ground nutmeg
- ❖ 1¼ grams hot paprika
- ❖ 60 milliliters olive oil
- ❖ 30 milliliters fresh lemon juice

Directions:

1. Ina large bowl, add all the ingredients except for chops and mix until well combined.
2. Add the chops and coat with the mixture generously.
3. Refrigerate to marinate for about 5-6 hours.
4. Preheat the gas grill to high heat. Grease the grill grate.
5. Place the lamb chops onto the grill and cook for about 6-8 minutes, flipping once halfway through.
6. Serve hot.

Lemony Lamb Chops

Servings|4   Time|18 minutes

Nutritional Content (per serving):

Cal| 476   Fat| 21.2g   Protein| 65.2g   Carbs| 1.7g

Ingredients:

- 2 garlic cloves, minced
- 15 milliliters olive oil
- Salt and ground black pepper, as required
- 15 grams Parmesan cheese, shredded
- 5 grams fresh oregano, minced
- 5 grams lemon zest, grated finely
- 30 milliliters fresh lemon juice
- 8 (4-ounce) lamb loin chops, trimmed

Directions:

1. In a bowl, add all the ingredients except lamb chops and Parmesan and mix until well combined.
2. Add the chops and coat with garlic mixture generously.
3. Cover and refrigerate to marinate for at least 1 hour.
4. Preheat the broiler of oven to high heat. Grease a broiler pan.
5. Arrange the chops onto the broiler pan.
6. Broil for about 3-4 minutes per side.
7. Serve hot with the sprinkling of the Parmesan.

Braised Lamb Shanks

Servings|6   Time|3¼ hours minutes

Nutritional Content (per serving):

Cal| 765   Fat| 27.5g   Protein| 84.2g   Carbs| 18.5g

Ingredients:

- ❖ 6 lamb shanks
- ❖ 30 milliliters olive oil
- ❖ 2 onions, chopped
- ❖ 1 (225-gram) can whole peeled tomatoes with juice
- ❖ 1 (680-gram) can beef broth
- ❖ 5 grams fresh rosemary, chopped
- ❖ Salt and ground black pepper, as required
- ❖ 3 carrots, peeled and chopped
- ❖ 10 garlic cloves, minced
- ❖ 1 (750-milliliter) bottle red wine
- ❖ 1 (295-gram) can condensed chicken soup
- ❖ 5 grams fresh thyme, chopped

Directions:

1. Season the shanks with salt and black pepper.
2. In a Dutch oven, heat the oil over medium-high heat and cook the shanks in 2 in batches for about 8 minutes or until browned from all sides.
3. With a slotted spoon, transfer the shanks onto a plate.
4. In the same pan, add the carrots, onions and garlic and cook for about 10 minutes, stirring frequently.
5. Add the remaining ingredients and stir to combine.
6. Add the shanks and bring to a boil.
7. Adjust the heat to medium-low and simmer, covered for about 2 hours.
8. Uncover the pan and simmer for about 20 minutes.
9. With a slotted spoon, transfer the shanks onto a platter and cover with a piece of foil to keep warm.
10. Place the pan over medium heat and cook for about 15 minutes or until thickened.
11. Pour sauce over shanks and serve.

Spiced Leg of Lamb

Servings|8   Time|1¾ hours

Nutritional Content (per serving):

Cal| 570   Fat| 43.9g   Protein| 42.2g   Carbs| 2.1g

Ingredients:

- 15 grams fresh parsley, minced
- 5 grams lemon zest, grated
- 10 grams ground cumin
- 10 grams red pepper flakes, crushed
- 2¼ kilograms bone-in leg of lamb, trimmed
- 4 garlic cloves, minced
- 10 grams ground coriander
- 10 grams smoked paprika
- 1½ grams ground allspice
- 90 milliliters olive oil

Directions:

1. In a large bowl, add all the ingredients except leg of lamb and mix well.
2. Coat the leg of lamb with marinade mixture generously.
3. With a plastic wrap, cover the leg of lamb and refrigerate to marinate for about 6-8 hours.
4. Remove from refrigerator and keep in room temperature for about 30 minutes before roasting.
5. Preheat your oven to 180 degrees C. Arrange the oven rack in the center of oven.
6. Arrange a lightly greased rack in the roasting pan.
7. Place the leg of lamb over rack into the roasting pan.
8. Roast for about 1¼-1½ hours, rotating the pan once halfway through.
9. Remove from oven and place the leg of lamb onto a cutting board for about 10-15 minutes.
10. With a sharp knife, cut the leg of lamb into desired size slices and serve.

Lamb Pita Pockets

Servings|4   Time|21 minutes

Nutritional Content (per serving):

Cal| 373   Fat| 10.6g   Protein| 31.2g   Carbs| 40.6g

Ingredients:

- 2 garlic cloves, minced
- Salt and ground black pepper, as required
- 340 grams boneless leg of lamb, cut into bite-sized pieces
- 4 whole-wheat pita breads, halved and warmed
- 5 grams fresh rosemary, minced
- 10 milliliters olive oil
- 225 grams cucumber, chopped finely
- 200 grams tomato, chopped
- 5 grams fresh parsley, chopped

Directions:

1. In a bowl, mix together garlic, rosemary, salt and black pepper.
2. Add lamb pieces and toss to coat well.
3. In a large nonstick wok, heat oil over medium-high heat and sear the lamb pieces for about 5-6 minutes or until desired doneness.
4. Meanwhile, in a bowl, mix together the cucumber, tomato, parsley, salt and black pepper.
5. Place the lamb pieces and cucumber mixture between all the pitas evenly and serve immediately.

Fish & Seafood Recipes

Garlicky Salmon

Servings|4   Time|22 minutes

Nutritional Content (per serving):

Cal| 341   Fat| 20.7g   Protein| 33.9g   Carbs| 4.4g

Ingredients:

- ❖ 140 grams plain Greek yogurt
- ❖ 5 grams fresh dill, minced
- ❖ 15 milliliters extra-virgin olive oil
- ❖ Salt and ground black pepper, as required
- ❖ 5 grams fresh basil leaves

- ❖ 3 garlic cloves, minced
- ❖ 30 milliliters fresh lemon juice
- ❖ 11½ grams ground coriander
- ❖ 11½ grams ground cumin
- ❖ 4 (150-gram) skinless salmon fillets

Directions:

1. In a bowl, add all the ingredients except the salmon and basil and mix well.
2. Transfer half of the yogurt mixture into another bowl and reserve for serving.
3. In the bowl of the remaining yogurt mixture, add the salmon fillets and coat with the mixture well.
4. Refrigerate for about 25-30 minutes, flipping once halfway through.
5. Preheat the grill to medium-high heat. Lightly grease the grill grate.
6. Remove the salmon fillets from bowl and with the paper towels, discard the excess yogurt mixture.
7. Grill the salmon fillets for about 4-6 minutes per side.
8. Serve with the topping of the reserved yogurt mixture and basil.

Walnut Crusted Salmon

Servings|2   Time|35 minutes

Nutritional Content (per serving):

Cal| 622   Fat| 45.7g   Protein| 47.2g   Carbs| 9.7g

Ingredients:

- ❖ 100 grams walnuts
- ❖ 19 grams lemon rind, grated
- ❖ Ground black pepper, as required
- ❖ 4 (85-gram) salmon fillets
- ❖ 5 grams fresh dill, chopped
- ❖ 1½ grams garlic salt
- ❖ 15 grams butter, melted
- ❖ 60-80 grams Dijon mustard
- ❖ 20 milliliters fresh lemon juice

Directions:

1. Preheat your oven to 180 degrees C. Line a large baking sheet with parchment paper.
2. In a food processor, place the walnuts and pulse until chopped roughly.
3. Add the dill, lemon rind, garlic salt, black pepper, and butter and pulse until a crumbly mixture form.
4. Place the salmon fillets onto the prepared baking sheet in a single layer, skin-side down.
5. Coat the top of each salmon fillet with Dijon mustard.
6. Place the walnut mixture over each fillet and gently press into the surface of salmon.
7. Bake for approximately 15-20 minutes.
8. Remove the salmon fillets from oven and transfer onto the serving plates.
9. Drizzle with the lemon juice and serve.

Salmon with Avocado Cream

Servings|4   Time|23 minutes

Nutritional Content (per serving):

Cal| 606   Fat| 43.6g   Protein| 39.8g   Carbs| 17g

Ingredients:

For Avocado Cream:

- ❖ 2 avocados, peeled, pitted and chopped
- ❖ 280 grams Greek yogurt
- ❖ 2 garlic cloves, chopped
- ❖ 45-60 milliliters fresh lime juice
- ❖ 5 grams fresh dill, minced
- ❖ Salt and ground black pepper, as required

For Salmon:

- ❖ 10 grams ground cumin
- ❖ 10 grams red chili powder
- ❖ 10 grams garlic powder
- ❖ Salt and ground black pepper, as required
- ❖ 4 (150-gram) skinless salmon fillets
- ❖ 30 grams butter

Directions:

1. **For avocado cream:** in a food processor, add all the ingredients and pulse until smooth.
2. In a small bowl, mix together the spices.
3. Coat the salmon fillets with spice mixture evenly.
4. In a non-stick wok, melt butter over medium-high heat and cook salmon fillets for about 3 minutes.
5. Flip and cook for about 4-5 minutes or until desired doneness.
6. Transfer the salmon fillets onto serving plates.
7. Top with avocado cream and serve.

Salmon with Wine Sauce

Servings|4   Time|28 minutes

Nutritional Content (per serving):

Cal| 566   Fat| 46.5g   Protein| 29.9g   Carbs| 5.9g

Ingredients:

- 3¾ grams lemon pepper seasoning
- 4 (140-gram) salmon fillets
- 150 grams butter, divided
- 1 shallot, minced
- 15 milliliters white wine vinegar
- Salt and ground white pepper, as required
- 5 grams dried thyme
- 5 grams dried parsley
- 75 milliliters fresh lemon juice, divided
- 75 milliliters white wine, divided
- 250 grams half-and-half

Directions:

1. In a small bowl, mix together the lemon pepper seasoning and dried herbs.
2. In a shallow dish, place the salmon filets and rub with 45 milliliters of lemon juice.
3. Season the non-skin side with herb mixture. Set aside.
4. In a wok, melt 30 grams of butter over medium heat, and sauté the shallot for about 2 minutes.
5. Stir in the remaining lemon juice, 60 milliliters of wine and vinegar and simmer for about 2-3 minutes.
6. Stir in half-and-half, salt and white pepper and cook for about 2-3 minutes.
7. Add 60 grams of butter and beat until well combined.
8. Remove from the heat and set aside, covered to keep warm.
9. In a wok, melt remaining butter over medium heat.
10. Place the salmon in the wok, herb side down and cook for about 1-2 minutes.
11. Transfer the salmon fillets onto a plate, herb side up.
12. In the wok, add the remaining wine, scraping up the browned bits from bottom.
13. Place the salmon fillets into the wok, herb side up and cook for about 8 minutes.
14. Serve salmon with the topping of pan sauce.

Parmesan Tilapia

Servings|4   Time|21 minutes

Nutritional Content (per serving):

Cal| 292   Fat| 13.4g   Protein| 43.3g   Carbs| 0.5g

Ingredients:

- ❖ 4 (150-gram) tilapia filets
- ❖ Salt and ground black pepper, as required
- ❖ 55 grams Parmesan cheese, grated
- ❖ 30 grams butter, melted

Directions:

1. Preheat the broiler of oven. Line a baking sheet with a greased piece of foil
2. Season the tilapia fillets with salt and black pepper lightly.
3. Arrange the tilapia fillets onto the prepared baking sheet line in a single layer and top each with Parmesan cheese evenly.
4. Broil for about 10-11 minutes.
5. Remove from the oven and transfer the tilapia fillets onto the serving plates.
6. Drizzle with the melted butter and serve.

Tilapia Piccata

Servings|4   Time|18 minutes

Nutritional Content (per serving):

Cal| 191   Fat| 8.6g   Protein| 28.3g   Carbs| 1g

Ingredients:

- ❖ 45 milliliters fresh lemon juice
- ❖ 2 garlic cloves, minced
- ❖ 15 grams fresh basil, minced and divided
- ❖ 4 (150-gram) tilapia fillets
- ❖ 30 milliliters olive oil
- ❖ 1½ grams lemon zest, grated
- ❖ 10 grams capers, drained
- ❖ Salt and ground black pepper, as required

Directions:

1. Preheat the broiler of the oven. Arrange an oven rack about 4-inch from the heating element. Grease a broiler pan.
2. In a small bowl, add the lemon juice, oil, garlic and lemon zest and beat until well combined.
3. Add the capers and half of basil and stir to combine.
4. Reserve some of mixture in a small bowl.
5. Coat the fish fillets with remaining capers mixture and sprinkle with salt and black pepper.
6. Place the tilapia fillets onto the broiler pan and broil for about 3-4 minutes side.
7. Remove from the oven and place the fish fillets onto serving plates.
8. Drizzle with reserved capers mixture and serve with the garnishing of remaining basil.

Tilapia Casserole

Servings|4   Time|24 minutes

Nutritional Content (per serving):

Cal| 210   Fat| 5.7g   Protein| 32.3g   Carbs| 9.1g

Ingredients:

- ❖ 2 (395-gram) cans diced tomatoes with basil and garlic with juice
- ❖ 1½ grams red pepper flakes, crushed
- ❖ 70 grams feta cheese, crumbled
- ❖ 10 grams fresh parsley, chopped and divided
- ❖ 1¼ grams dried oregano
- ❖ 4 (150-gram) tilapia fillets
- ❖ 30 milliliters fresh lemon juice

Directions:

1. Preheat your oven to 200 degrees C.
2. In a shallow baking dish, add the tomatoes, half of the parsley, oregano and red pepper flakes and mix until well combined.
3. Arrange the tilapia fillets over the tomato mixture in a single layer and drizzle with the lemon juice.
4. Place some tomato mixture over the tilapia fillets and sprinkle with the feta cheese evenly.
5. Bake for approximately 12-14 minutes.
6. Serve hot with the garnishing of remaining parsley.

Cod in Tomato Sauce

Servings|5   Time|50 minutes

Nutritional Content (per serving):

Cal| 236   Fat| 7.5g   Protein| 33.6g   Carbs| 12g

Ingredients:

- 5 grams dried dill weed
- 10 grams ground coriander
- 5 grams ground turmeric
- 30 milliliters olive oil
- 8 garlic cloves, chopped
- 5 medium tomatoes, chopped
- 30 milliliters fresh lime juice
- Salt and ground black pepper, as required
- 10 grams sumac
- 11½ grams ground cumin
- 1 large onion, chopped
- 2 jalapeño peppers, chopped
- 45 grams tomato paste
- 120 milliliters water
- 5 (150-gram) cod fillets

Directions:

1. For spice mixture: in a small bowl, add the dill weed and spices and mix well.
2. In a large, deep wok, heat the oil over medium-high heat and sauté the onion for about 2 minutes.
3. Add the garlic and jalapeno and sauté for about 2 minutes.
4. Stir in the tomatoes, tomato paste, lime juice, water, half of the spice mixture, salt and pepper and bring to a boil.
5. Adjust the heat to medium-low and cook, covered for about 10 minutes, stirring occasionally.
6. Meanwhile, season the cod fillets with the remaining spice mixture, salt and pepper evenly.
7. Place the fish fillets into the wok and gently press into the tomato mixture.
8. Adjust the heat to medium-high and cook for about 2 minutes.
9. Adjust the heat to medium and cook, covered for about 10-15 minutes or until desired doneness of the fish.
10. Serve hot.

Halibut & Olives Parcel

Servings|4   Time|55 minutes

Nutritional Content (per serving):

Cal| 354   Fat| 21.7g   Protein| 32.9g   Carbs| 7.7g

Ingredients:

- ❖ 1 onion, chopped
- ❖ 1 (140-gram) jar pitted kalamata olives
- ❖ 15 milliliters fresh lemon juice
- ❖ 4 (150-gram) halibut fillets
- ❖ 10 grams Greek seasoning
- ❖ 1 large tomato, chopped
- ❖ 30 grams capers
- ❖ 60 milliliters olive oil
- ❖ Salt and ground black pepper, as required

Directions:

1. Preheat your oven to 180 degrees C.
2. In a bowl, add the onion, tomato, onion, olives, capers, oil, lemon juice, salt and black pepper and mix well.
3. Season the halibut fillets with the Greek seasoning and arrange onto a large piece of foil.
4. Top the fillets with the tomato mixture.
5. Carefully fold all the edges of to create a large packet.
6. Arrange the packet onto a baking sheet.
7. Bake for approximately 30-40 minutes.
8. Serve hot.

Tuna with Olives Sauce

Servings|4   Time|25 minutes

Nutritional Content (per serving):

Cal| 438   Fat| 19.9g   Protein| 46.1g   Carbs| 7.3g

Ingredients:

- ❖ 4 (150-gram) tuna steaks
- ❖ Salt and ground black pepper, as required
- ❖ 240 milliliters dry white wine
- ❖ 30 grams capers, drained
- ❖ 5 grams lemon zest, grated
- ❖ 10 grams fresh parsley, chopped
- ❖ 30 milliliters olive oil, divided
- ❖ 2 garlic cloves, minced
- ❖ 1 large tomato, chopped
- ❖ 115 grams olives, pitted and sliced
- ❖ 5 grams fresh thyme, chopped
- ❖ 30 milliliters fresh lemon juice

Directions:

1. Preheat the grill to high heat. Grease the grill grate.
2. Coat the tuna steaks with 15 milliliters of the oil and sprinkle with salt and black pepper. Set aside for about 5 minutes.
3. For sauce: in a small wok, heat the remaining oil over medium heat and sauté the garlic for about 1 minute.
4. Add the tomatoes and cook for about 2 minutes.
5. Stir in the wine and bring to a boil.
6. Add the remaining ingredients except the parsley and cook, uncovered for about 5 minutes.
7. Stir in the parsley, salt and black pepper and remove from the heat.
8. Meanwhile, grill the tuna steaks over direct heat for about 1-2 minutes per side.
9. Serve the tuna steaks hot with the topping of sauce.

Shrimp with Zoodles

Servings|4   Time|25 minutes

Nutritional Content (per serving):

Cal| 207   Fat| 8.2g   Protein| 26.5g   Carbs| 9.5g

Ingredients:

- 30 grams butter
- Salt and ground black pepper, as required
- 2 large courgettes, spiralized with Blade C
- 5 grams fresh lemon zest, grated
- 30 grams Parmesan cheese, grated
- 455 grams large shrimp, peeled and deveined
- 1¼ grams red pepper flakes
- 4 garlic cloves, minced
- 30 milliliters fresh lemon juice
- 60 milliliters chicken broth
- 15 grams fresh parsley, chopped

Directions:

1. In a large wok, melt the butter over medium-low heat and sauté the shrimp, salt, black pepper and red pepper flakes for about 4-6 minutes.
2. Stir in the garlic and cook for about 1 minute, stirring frequently.
3. Stir in the courgette noodles, lemon juice, zest and broth and bring to a boil.
4. Cook for about 1 minute.
5. Serve hot with the topping of Parmesan and parsley.

Shrimp Casserole

Servings|6   Time|45 minutes
Nutritional Content (per serving):
Cal| 298   Fat| 14.4g   Protein| 29.4g   Carbs| 6.8g

Ingredients:

- 60 grams butter
- 680 grams large shrimp, peeled and deveined
- 1¼ grams red pepper flakes, crushed
- 1 (410-gram) can diced tomatoes
- 1 garlic clove, minced
- 3¾ grams dried oregano, crushed
- 15 grams fresh coriander, chopped
- 180 milliliters dry vermouth
- 115 grams feta cheese, crumbled

Directions:

1. Preheat your oven to 180 degrees C.
2. In a large wok, melt butter over medium-high heat.
3. Add the garlic and sauté for about 1 minute.
4. Add the shrimp, oregano and red pepper flakes and cook for about 4-5 minutes.
5. Stir in the parsley and salt and immediately transfer into a casserole dish evenly.
6. In the same wok, add vermouth on medium heat. Simmer for about 2-3 minutes or until reduces to half.
7. Stir in tomatoes and cook for about 2-3 minutes.
8. Pour the tomato mixture over shrimp mixture evenly.
9. Top with cheese evenly.
10. Bake for approximately 15-20 minutes or until top becomes golden brown.
11. Serve hot.

Octopus in Honey Sauce

Servings|8   Time|1 hour 25 minutes

Nutritional Content (per serving):

Cal| 216   Fat| 8.5g   Protein| 22.7g   Carbs| 7.8g

Ingredients:

- ❖ 1025 grams fresh octopus, washed
- ❖ 60 milliliters olive oil
- ❖ Pinch of saffron threads, crushed
- ❖ 20 grams tomato paste
- ❖ 20 grams honey
- ❖ Salt and ground black pepper, as required
- ❖ 1 bay leaf
- ❖ 90 milliliters water
- ❖ 2 onions, chopped finely
- ❖ 1 garlic clove, chopped finely
- ❖ 1 (395-gram) can diced tomatoes
- ❖ 180 milliliters red wine
- ❖ 15 grams fresh basil, chopped

Directions:

1. Remove the eyes of the octopus and cut out the beak.
2. Then, clean the head thoroughly.
3. In a deep pan, add the octopus, bay leaf and water over medium heat and cook for about 20 minutes.
4. Add the wine and simmer for about 50 minutes.
5. Meanwhile, for sauce: in a wok, heat the oil over medium heat and sauté the onions and saffron for about 3-4 minutes.
6. Add the garlic and tomato paste and sauté for about 1-2 minutes.
7. Stir in the tomatoes and honey and simmer for about 10 minutes.
8. Transfer the sauce into the pan of octopus and cooking for about 15 minutes.
9. Serve hot with the garnishing of basil.

Mussels in Wine Sauce

Servings|6   Time|30 minutes

Nutritional Content (per serving):

Cal| 261   Fat| 6.3g   Protein| 19.8g   Carbs| 17.2g

Ingredients:

- 15 milliliters olive oil
- 1 onion, chopped
- 1 (425-gram) can diced tomatoes
- 10 grams honey
- 910 grams mussels, cleaned
- Salt and ground black pepper, as required
- 450 grams celery stalks, chopped
- 4 garlic cloves, minced
- 1½ grams dried oregano
- 5 grams red pepper flakes
- 480 milliliters white wine
- 15 grams fresh basil, chopped

Directions:

1. In a wok, heat the oil over medium heat and sauté the celery, onion and garlic for about 5 minutes.
2. Add the tomato, honey and red pepper flakes and cook for about 10 minutes.
3. Meanwhile, in a large pan, add mussels and wine and bring to a boil.
4. Simmer, covered for about 10 minutes.
5. Transfer the mussel mixture into tomato mixture and stir to combine.
6. Season with salt and black pepper and remove from the heat.
7. Serve hot with the garnishing of basil.

Seafood Paella

Servings|4   Time|1 hour

Nutritional Content (per serving):

Cal| 494   Fat| 7.7g   Protein| 31.6g   Carbs| 72.8g

Ingredients:

- 15 milliliters olive oil
- 1 capsicum, seeded and chopped
- 1 large onion, chopped finely
- 290 grams short-grain rice
- 5 grams paprika
- 2 pinches saffron threads, crushed
- 12 mussels, cleaned
- 12 large shrimp, peeled and deveined
- 4 garlic cloves, minced
- 1½ grams ground turmeric
- 150 grams canned diced tomatoes
- 720 milliliters chicken broth
- 70 grams frozen green peas, thawed
- 15 grams fresh coriander, chopped
- 1 lemon, cut into wedges

Directions:

1. In a deep pan, heat oil over medium-high heat and sauté the capsicum, onion and garlic for about 3 minutes.
2. Add the rice, turmeric and paprika and stir to combine.
3. Stir in the tomatoes, saffron and broth and bring to a boil.
4. Adjust the heat to low and simmer, covered for about 20 minutes.
5. Place the mussels, shrimp and peas on top and simmer, covered for about 10-15 minutes.
6. Serve hot with the garnishing of parsley and lemon wedges.

Salad, Soup & Stews Recipes

Watermelon Salad

Servings|6   Time|15 minutes

Nutritional Content (per serving):

Cal| 124   Fat| 4.6g   Protein| 2.6g   Carbs| 20.5g

Ingredients:

For Vinaigrette:

- 30 milliliters fresh lime juice
- 40 grams honey
- 15 milliliters olive oil
- Pinch of salt
- Pinch of ground black pepper

For Salad:

- 1 (2¼-kilogram) watermelon, peeled and cut into cubes
- 1 red onion, sliced
- 5 grams fresh mint, torn
- 55 grams feta cheese, crumbled

Directions:

1. For vinaigrette: in a small bowl, all the ingredients and beat until well combined.
2. In a large bowl, add the watermelon, onion and mint and mix.
3. Place the vinaigrette and gently toss to coat.
4. Top with the feta cheese and serve.

Caprese Salad

Servings|4   Time|15 minutes

Nutritional Content (per serving):

Cal| 175   Fat| 15.7g   Protein| 4.1g   Carbs| 7.1g

Ingredients:

For Dressing:

- 20 grams fresh basil, chopped
- 2 garlic cloves, minced
- 60 milliliters extra-virgin olive oil
- 30 milliliters balsamic vinegar
- Salt and ground black pepper, as required

For Salad:

- 4 medium ripe tomatoes, cut into slices
- 85 grams fresh mozzarella cheese, cubed
- 150 grams fresh baby spinach

Directions:

1. For dressing: in a small blender, add all the ingredients and pulse until smooth.
2. For salad: in a large bowl, add all the ingredients and mix.
3. Place the dressing over salad and toss to coat well.
4. Serve immediately.

Chicken Salad

Servings|6   Time|15 minutes

Nutritional Content (per serving):

Cal| 277   Fat| 11.6g   Protein| 33.4g   Carbs| 9.2g

Ingredients:

For Dressing:

- ❖ 70 grams plain Greek yogurt
- ❖ 60 grams Dijon mustard
- ❖ 16 grams sunflower seeds
- ❖ 5 grams kelp powder
- ❖ 1½ grams ground turmeric
- ❖ 1¼ grams ground cumin
- ❖ 1¼ grams onion powder
- ❖ 1¼ grams garlic powder
- ❖ Salt and ground black pepper, as required

For Salad:

- ❖ 600 grams cooked chicken breasts, shredded
- ❖ 165 grams fresh baby kale
- ❖ 90 grams fresh baby spinach
- ❖ 2-3 celery stalks, chopped
- ❖ 5 grams fresh parsley, chopped
- ❖ 55 grams dried cherries
- ❖ 25 grams almonds, chopped

Directions:

1. For dressing: in a bowl, add all ingredients and beat until well combined.
2. For salad: in a large serving bowl, add all the ingredients and mix.
3. Place dressing over the salad and gently toss to coat.
4. Serve immediately.

Tuna Salad

Servings|6   Time|15 minutes

Nutritional Content (per serving):

Cal| 314   Fat| 22g   Protein| 20.5g   Carbs| 11g

Ingredients:

For Vinaigrette:

- ❖ 45 milliliters fresh lime juice
- ❖ 90 milliliters extra-virgin olive oil
- ❖ 10 grams Dijon mustard
- ❖ 5 grams lime zest, grated
- ❖ 1½ grams red pepper flakes
- ❖ Salt and ground black pepper, as required

For Salad:

- ❖ 3 (140-gram) cans tuna
- ❖ 1 red onion, chopped
- ❖ 2 cucumbers, sliced
- ❖ 1 large tomato, sliced
- ❖ 90 grams Kalamata olives, pitted
- ❖ 600 grams lettuce leaves, torn
- ❖ 15 grams fresh basil leaves

Directions:

1. For vinaigrette: in a bowl, add all the ingredients and beat until well combined.
2. For salad: in a large serving bowl, add all the ingredients and mix.
3. Place the dressing over the salad and gently toss to coat.
4. Refrigerate, covered for about 30-40 minutes before serving.

Tomato Soup

Servings|8   Time|43 minutes

Nutritional Content (per serving):

Cal| 129   Fat| 8.2g   Protein| 6.6g   Carbs| 8.7g

Ingredients:

- 45 milliliters olive oil
- Salt, as required
- 5 grams ground cumin
- 1 (425-gram) can diced tomatoes with juice
- 1 (225-gram) can plum tomatoes with juices
- 2 medium onions, sliced thinly
- 15 grams curry powder
- 5 grams ground coriander
- 1½ grams red pepper flakes
- 1320 milliliters vegetable broth
- 125 grams ricotta cheese, crumbled

Directions:

1. In a Dutch oven, heat the oil over medium-low heat and cook the onion with 5 grams of the salt for about 12 minutes, stirring occasionally.
2. Stir in the curry powder, cumin, coriander and red pepper flakes and sauté for about 1 minute.
3. Stir in the tomatoes with juices and broth and simmer for about 15 minutes.
4. Remove from the heat and with a hand blender, blend the soup until smooth.
5. Serve immediately with the topping of ricotta cheese.

Chicken & Orzo Soup

Servings|8   Time|35 minutes

Nutritional Content (per serving):

Cal| 231   Fat| 7.2g   Protein| 25.9g   Carbs| 13.4g

Ingredients:

- ❖ 15 milliliters olive oil
- ❖ 10 grams Greek seasoning
- ❖ Salt and ground black pepper, as required
- ❖ 60 milliliters white wine
- ❖ 15 grams sun-dried tomatoes, chopped
- ❖ 5 grams fresh oregano, minced
- ❖ 5 grams fresh parsley, chopped

- ❖ 680 grams skinless, boneless chicken breasts, cubed
- ❖ 4 green onions, sliced thinly
- ❖ 1 garlic clove, minced
- ❖ 45 grams olives, pitted and sliced
- ❖ 10 grams capers, drained
- ❖ 5 grams fresh basil, minced
- ❖ 1680 milliliters chicken broth
- ❖ 150 grams uncooked orzo pasta
- ❖ 30 milliliters fresh lemon juice

Directions:

1. In a Dutch oven, heat oil over medium heat and cook chicken with Greek seasoning and black pepper for about 4-5 minutes or until golden brown from both sides.
2. With a slotted spoon, transfer the chicken breasts onto a plate and set aside.
3. In the same pan, add the green onions and garlic and sauté for about 1 minute.
4. Add the wine and scrape out the brown bits from the bottom of pan.
5. Stir in the cooked chicken, olives, tomatoes, capers, oregano, basil and broth and bring to a boil.
6. Adjust the heat to low and simmer, covered for about 15 minutes.
7. Adjust the heat to medium and again bring to a boil.
8. Stir in orzo and cook for about 8-10 minutes or until desired doneness of the pasta.
9. Stir in the lemon juice and parsley and serve hot.

Lentil & Quinoa Soup

Servings|4   Time|1¼ hours

Nutritional Content (per serving):

Cal| 320   Fat| 3.9g   Protein| 17.8g   Carbs| 56.3g

Ingredients:

- ❖ 95 grams quinoa, rinsed
- ❖ 50 grams fresh mushrooms, sliced
- ❖ 225 grams celery stalk, chopped
- ❖ 10 grams ground ginger
- ❖ 5 grams red chili powder
- ❖ 5 grams fresh coriander, chopped
- ❖ 210 grams dry lentils, rinsed
- ❖ 60 grams carrot, peeled and chopped
- ❖ 10 grams ground cumin
- ❖ 5 grams red pepper flakes
- ❖ 960 milliliters water

Directions:

1. In a large soup pan, mix together all ingredients except coriander over high heat and bring to a boil.
2. Adjust the heat to medium-low and simmer, covered for about 1 hour or until lentil becomes tender.
3. Serve hot with the garnishing of coriander.

Turkey Meatballs Soup

Servings|6   Time|40 minutes

Nutritional Content (per serving):

Cal| 244   Fat| 13.6g   Protein| 26.8g   Carbs| 3.8g

Ingredients:

For Meatballs:

- ❖ 455 grams lean ground turkey
- ❖ 1 garlic clove, minced finely
- ❖ 1 egg, beaten
- ❖ 30 grams Parmesan cheese, grated freshly
- ❖ Salt and ground black pepper, as required

For Soup:

- ❖ 15 milliliters olive oil
- ❖ 1 small onion, chopped finely
- ❖ 1 garlic clove, minced
- ❖ 1440 milliliters chicken broth
- ❖ 180 grams fresh spinach, chopped
- ❖ 2 eggs, beaten lightly
- ❖ 30 grams Parmesan cheese, grated
- ❖ Salt and ground black pepper, as required

Directions:

1. For meatballs: in a bowl, add all the ingredients and mix until well combined.
2. Make small equal-sized balls from the mixture.
3. In a large soup pan, heat the oil over medium heat and sauté the onion for about 5-6 minutes.
4. Add the garlic and sauté for about 1 minute.
5. Add the broth and bring to a boil.
6. Carefully place the balls in pan and bring to a boil.
7. Adjust the heat to low and simmer for about 10 minutes.
8. Stir in the spinach and bring to a gentle simmer.
9. Simmer for about 2-3 minutes.
10. Slowly, add the beaten eggs, stirring continuously.
11. Stir in the cheese until melted.
12. Season with salt and black pepper and serve hot.

Pork Stew

Servings|6   Time|3 hours 35 minutes

Nutritional Content (per serving):

Cal| 752   Fat| 34.5g   Protein| 64.7g   Carbs| 62.6g

Ingredients:

- ❖ 455 grams dried Great Northern beans
- ❖ 1 (395-gram) can crushed tomatoes
- ❖ 225 grams partially cooked garlic sausage, sliced
- ❖ 225 grams bacon, cut into ½-inch chunks
- ❖ Salt and ground black pepper, as required
- ❖ 720 milliliters chicken broth
- ❖ 1 onion, cut into chunks
- ❖ 365 grams carrots, peeled and chopped
- ❖ 455 grams pork shoulder, cut into 1-inch chunks
- ❖ 5 grams fresh parsley
- ❖ 5 grams fresh thyme
- ❖ 5 grams ground allspice
- ❖ 240 milliliters red wine

Directions:

1. Preheat your oven to 120 degrees C.
2. In a large pan of water, add the beans and cook for about 20 minutes.
3. Remove from the heat and drain the beans.
4. In a large casserole dish, place the beans and remaining all ingredients except for wine and stir to combine.
5. Cover the casserole dish and bake for approximately 2 hours.
6. Uncover and stir in the wine.
7. Bake for approximately 1 hour more.
8. Serve hot.

Seafood Stew

Servings|4   Time|40 minutes

Nutritional Content (per serving):

Cal| 470   Fat| 11.8g   Protein| 66.4g   Carbs| 17g

Ingredients:

- ❖ 30 milliliters olive oil
- ❖ 2 garlic cloves, minced
- ❖ 225 grams tomatoes, chopped finely
- ❖ 20 grams tomato paste
- ❖ 455 grams snapper fillets, cubed
- ❖ 455 grams shrimp, peeled and deveined
- ❖ 1 medium onion, chopped finely
- ❖ 1¼ grams red pepper flakes
- ❖ 90 milliliters white wine
- ❖ 240 milliliters clam juice
- ❖ Salt, as required
- ❖ 225 grams sea scallops
- ❖ 15 grams fresh coriander, minced
- ❖ 5 grams lemon zest, grated

Directions:

1. In a Dutch oven, heat oil over medium heat and sauté the onion for about 3-4 minutes.
2. Add the garlic and red pepper flakes and sauté for about 1 minute.
3. Add the tomatoes and cook for about 2 minutes.
4. Stir in the wine, clam juice, tomato paste and salt and bring to a boil.
5. Adjust the heat to low and simmer, covered for about 10 minutes.
6. Stir in the seafood and simmer, covered for about 6-8 minutes.
7. Stir in the parsley and remove from heat.
8. Serve hot with the garnishing of lemon zest.

Beans & Farro Stew

Servings|6   Time|1 hour

Nutritional Content (per serving):

Cal| 326   Fat| 9.2g   Protein| 15.6g   Carbs| 45g

Ingredients:

- ❖ 30 milliliters olive oil
- ❖ 2 celery stalks, chopped
- ❖ 4 garlic cloves, minced
- ❖ 190 grams farro, rinsed
- ❖ 1 bay leaf
- ❖ 1 (425-gram) can cannellini beans, drained and rinsed
- ❖ 55 grams feta cheese, crumbled
- ❖ 1 carrot, peeled and chopped
- ❖ 120 grams onion, chopped
- ❖ 1 (410-gram) can diced tomatoes
- ❖ 3 fresh parsley sprigs
- ❖ 1200 milliliters vegetable broth
- ❖ 220 grams fresh kale, chopped
- ❖ 15 milliliters fresh lemon juice

Directions:

1. In a saucepan, heat the oil over medium-high heat and sauté the carrots, celery and onion for about 3 minutes.
2. Add the garlic and sauté for about 30 seconds.
3. Add tomatoes, farro, parsley, bay leaf, salt and broth and bring to a boil.
4. Adjust the heat to medium-low and simmer covered for about 20 minutes.
5. With a slotted spoon, remove the parsley sprigs and discard them.
6. Stir in the kale and cook for about 10-15 minutes or until desired doneness.
7. Stir in the cannellini beans and cook for about 1-2 minutes.
8. Stir in the lemon juice and serve hot with the topping of feta cheese.

Chickpeas Stew

Servings|3   Time|50 minutes

Nutritional Content (per serving):

Cal| 253   Fat| 7.4g   Protein| 9.5g   Carbs| 40.1g

Ingredients:

- 15 milliliters olive oil
- 3 green onions, sliced
- 1½ grams ground cumin
- 1 (225-gram) can whole, peeled tomatoes, crushed
- Salt and ground black pepper, as required
- 400 grams canned chickpeas
- 1 capsicum, seeded and julienned
- 2 garlic cloves, minced
- 1½ grams paprika
- Pinch of brown sugar
- 120 milliliters vegetable broth
- 5 grams fresh parsley, minced

Directions:

1. In a saucepan, heat the oil over medium heat and sauté the capsicum, green onions, garlic, pan, cumin and paprika for about 4-5 minutes.
2. Stir in the tomatoes, brown sugar, salt, black pepper and broth and simmer for about 20 minutes.
3. Stir in the chickpeas and parsley and simmer for about 10 minutes.
4. Serve hot.

Vegetarian Recipes

Stuffed Tomatoes

Servings|2   Time|20 minutes

Nutritional Content (per serving):

Cal| 210   Fat| 13.9g   Protein| 5.5g   Carbs| 16.7g

Ingredients:

- ❖ 2 large tomatoes, halved crosswise
- ❖ 10 grams fresh basil, chopped
- ❖ 30 milliliters balsamic vinaigrette
- ❖ 45 grams kalamata olives, pitted and sliced
- ❖ 30 grams feta cheese, crumbled
- ❖ 20 grams garlic croutons

Directions:

1. Preheat the broiler of the oven. Arrange the oven rack about 4-5-nch from the heating element.
2. With your fingers, remove the seeds from the tomato halves.
3. Carefully run a small knife around the pulp vertically, not touching the bottom and then, gently remove the pulp.
4. Chop the tomato pulp and transfer into a bowl.
5. Arrange the tomatoes over the paper towels, cut side down to drain.
6. In the bowl of tomato pulp, add the remaining ingredients and mix well.
7. Stuff the tomatoes with olive mixture evenly.
8. Arrange the tomatoes onto a broiler pan and broil for about 5 minutes or until cheese is melted
9. Serve warm.

Stuffed Courgette

Servings|8   Time|33 minutes

Nutritional Content (per serving):

Cal| 61   Fat| 3g   Protein| 2.9g   Carbs| 7.3g

Ingredients:

- ❖ 4 medium courgettes, halved lengthwise
- ❖ 90 grams Kalamata olives, pitted and minced
- ❖ 5 grams dried oregano, crushed
- ❖ 55 grams feta cheese, crumbled
- ❖ 175 grams capsicum, seeded and minced
- ❖ 100 grams tomatoes, minced
- ❖ 5 grams garlic, minced
- ❖ Salt and ground black pepper, as required

Directions:

1. Preheat your oven to 180 degrees C. Grease a large baking sheet.
2. With a melon baller, scoop out the flesh of each courgette half. Discard the flesh.
3. In a bowl, mix together capsicum, olives, tomato, garlic, oregano and black pepper.
4. Stuff each courgette half with veggie mixture evenly.
5. Arrange courgette halves onto the prepared baking sheet and bake for approximately 15 minutes.
6. Now, set the oven to broiler on high.
7. Top each courgette half with feta cheese and broil for about 3 minutes.
8. Serve hot.

Ratatouille

Servings|4   Time|1 hour

Nutritional Content (per serving):

Cal| 199   Fat| 11.5g   Protein| 5g   Carbs| 24.5g

Ingredients:

- ❖ 150 grams tomato paste
- ❖ ½ onion, chopped
- ❖ Salt and ground black pepper, as required
- ❖ 2 courgettes, cut into thin circles
- ❖ 2 capsicums, seeded and cut into circles thinly
- ❖ 45 milliliters olive oil, divided
- ❖ 3 garlic cloves, minced
- ❖ 180 milliliters water
- ❖ 1 brinjal, cut into circles thinly
- ❖ 5 grams fresh thyme, minced
- ❖ 15 milliliters fresh lemon juice

Directions:

1. Preheat your oven to 190 degrees C.
2. In a bowl, add the tomato paste, 15 milliliters of oil, onion, garlic, salt and black pepper and blend nicely.
3. In the bottom of a 10x10-inch baking dish, spread the tomato paste mixture evenly.
4. Arrange alternating vegetable slices, starting at the outer edge of the baking dish and working concentrically towards the center.
5. Drizzle the vegetables with the remaining oil and sprinkle with salt and black pepper, followed by the thyme.
6. Arrange a piece of parchment paper over the vegetables.
7. Bake for approximately 45 minutes.
8. Serve hot.

Curried Veggies Bake

Servings|6   Time|35 minutes

Nutritional Content (per serving):

Cal| 78   Fat| 5.3g   Protein| 1.9g   Carbs| 8g

Ingredients:

- ❖ 1 medium courgette, chopped
- ❖ 2 capsicums, seeded and cubed
- ❖ 1 yellow onion, sliced thinly
- ❖ 10 grams curry powder
- ❖ 60 milliliters vegetable broth
- ❖ 1 medium yellow squash, chopped
- ❖ 30 milliliters olive oil
- ❖ Salt and ground black pepper, as required
- ❖ 10 grams fresh coriander, chopped

Directions:

1. Preheat your oven to 190 degrees C. Lightly, grease a large baking dish.
2. In a large bowl, add all ingredients except for coriander and mix until well combined.
3. Transfer the vegetable mixture into the prepared baking dish.
4. Bake for approximately 15-20 minutes.
5. Serve immediately with the garnishing of coriander.

Parmesan Veggie Bake

Servings|4   Time|1 hour 5 minutes

Nutritional Content (per serving):

Cal| 207   Fat| 12.1g   Protein| 17.6g   Carbs| 8.3g

Ingredients:

- 4 large eggs
- 60 grams mozzarella cheese, shredded
- 5 grams garlic powder
- 2 medium capsicums, halved and seeded
- 70 grams Parmesan cheese, grated and divided
- 125 grams ricotta cheese
- 1¼ grams dried parsley
- 10 grams fresh baby spinach leaves

Directions:

1. Preheat your oven to 190 degrees C. Lightly grease a baking dish.
2. In a small food processor, place the eggs, 50 grams of Parmesan, mozzarella, ricotta cheese, garlic powder and parsley and pulse until well combined.
3. Arrange the capsicum halves into the prepared baking dish, cut side up.
4. Place the cheese mixture into each pepper half and top each with few spinach leaves.
5. With a fork, push the spinach leaves into cheese mixture.
6. With a piece of foil, cover the baking dish and bake for approximately 35-45 minutes.
7. Now, set the oven to broiler on high.
8. Top each capsicum half with the remaining Parmesan cheese and broil for about 3-5 minutes.
9. Remove from the oven and serve hot.

Couscous with Cauliflower & Dates

Servings|4   Time|55 minutes

Nutritional Content (per serving):

Cal| 329   Fat| 15.1g   Protein| 7.9g   Carbs| 42g

Ingredients:

- 170 grams cauliflower florets
- Salt and ground black pepper, as required
- 165 grams pearl couscous
- 40 grams dates, pitted and chopped
- 60 milliliters olive oil, divided
- 2 garlic cloves, minced
- 300 milliliters vegetable broth
- 15 milliliters fresh lemon juice
- 5 milliliters red wine vinegar

Directions:

1. Preheat your oven to 200 degrees C. Line a baking sheet with parchment paper.
2. In a bowl, add cauliflower, 30 milliliters of oil, salt and black pepper and mix well.
3. Arrange the cauliflower onto the prepared baking sheet and spread in an even layer.
4. Roast for about 35-40 minutes or until the cauliflower is golden.
5. Remove the cauliflower from the oven and set aside to cool for about 10 minutes.
6. Meanwhile, for couscous: in a pan, heat 15 milliliters of oil over medium-high heat and sauté the garlic for about 1 minute.
7. Add the broth and bring to a boil.
8. Stir in couscous and adjust the heat to medium.
9. Cover the pan and simmer for about 8-10 minutes, stirring occasionally.
10. Stir in the lemon juice and remove from the heat.
11. Meanwhile, in a wok, heat the remaining oil over medium heat and sauté the shallot for about 6 minutes.
12. Stir in the dates and cook for about 2 minutes.
13. Stir in the vinegar, salt and black pepper and remove from the heat.
14. Transfer the date mixture into the pan with the couscous and stir to combine.
15. In a large serving bowl, add the couscous and cauliflower and gently stir to combine.
16. Serve warm.

Lentil & Quinoa Casserole

Servings|4   Time|1 hour 5 minutes

Nutritional Content (per serving):

Cal| 603   Fat| 22.6g   Protein| 30.3g   Carbs| 72.8g

Ingredients:

- ❖ 30 milliliters olive oil
- ❖ 3 garlic cloves, minced
- ❖ 485 grams cooked quinoa
- ❖ 300 grams cherry tomatoes, halved
- ❖ 140 grams plain Greek yogurt
- ❖ Salt and ground black pepper, as required
- ❖ 1 large onion, chopped
- ❖ 285 grams fresh baby spinach
- ❖ 210 grams cooked brown lentils
- ❖ 2 medium eggs
- ❖ 150 grams feta cheese, crumbled
- ❖ 15 grams fresh dill, chopped

Directions:

1. Preheat your oven to 190 degrees C. Grease a 9x13-inch casserole dish.
2. In a large wok, heat the oil over medium heat and sauté the onion and garlic for about 3-5 minutes.
3. Stir in the spinach and cook, covered for about 2½ minutes.
4. Uncover and cook for about 2½ minutes.
5. With a slotted spoon, transfer the spinach mixture onto a paper towel-lined plate to drain.
6. In a bowl, add the quinoa, lentils, spinach mixture and tomatoes and mix.
7. In another bowl, add the yogurt, eggs, feta, dill, salt and black pepper and mix until well combined.
8. Add the quinoa mixture and mix until well combined.
9. Place the mixture into the prepared casserole dish evenly.
10. Bake for approximately 35-40 minutes or until top becomes golden brown.
11. Remove from the oven and set aside to cool for about 10 minutes before serving.

Beans & Rice in Sauce

Servings|4   Time|30 minutes

Nutritional Content (per serving):

Cal| 432   Fat| 6.1g   Protein| 18.6g   Carbs| 76.5g

Ingredients:

- ❖ 1 (425-gram) can cannellini beans, rinsed and drained
- ❖ 135 grams uncooked instant rice
- ❖ 240 milliliters vegetable broth
- ❖ 5 grams Italian seasoning
- ❖ 30 grams Parmesan cheese, grated
- ❖ 1 (425-gram) can chickpeas, rinsed and drained
- ❖ 1 (410-gram) can stewed tomatoes with juice
- ❖ 1¼ grams red pepper flakes
- ❖ 300 grams marinara sauce

Directions:

1. In a non-stick wok, add all ingredients except for marinara and Parmesan and stir to combine.
2. Place the pan over medium-high heat and bring to a boil.
3. Adjust the heat to low and simmer, covered or about 7-9 minutes or until rice is tender.
4. Stir in the marinara sauce and cook for about 2-3 minutes or until heated through, stirring occasionally.
5. Top with cheese and serve.

Asparagus Risotto

Servings|4   Time|1 hour

Nutritional Content (per serving):

Cal| 303   Fat| 10.4g   Protein| 13.2g   Carbs| 34.9g

Ingredients:

- 15-20 asparagus spears, trimmed and chopped
- 1 garlic clove, minced
- 5 grams lemon zest, grated
- 120 milliliters white wine
- Salt and ground black pepper, as required
- 30 milliliters vegetable oil
- 120 grams onion, chopped
- 130 grams Arborio rice
- 30 milliliters fresh lemon juice
- 1200 milliliters hot vegetable broth
- 30 grams Parmesan cheese, shredded

Directions:

1. In a medium pan of boiling water, add the asparagus and cook for about 2-3 minutes.
2. Drain the asparagus and rinse under cold water. Set aside.
3. In a large pan, heat oil over medium heat and sauté the onion and garlic for about 4-5 minutes.
4. Add the rice and stir fry for about 2 minutes.
5. Add the lemon zest, juice and white wine and cook for about 2-3 minutes or until all the liquid is absorbed, stirring gently.
6. Add 240 milliners of broth and cook until all the broth is absorbed, stirring occasionally.
7. Repeat this process by adding 180 milliliters of broth at once, stirring occasionally. (This procedure will take about 20-30 minutes)
8. Stir in the cooked asparagus and remaining ingredients and cook for about 3-4 minutes.
9. Serve hot.

Chickpeas Falafel

Servings|6   Time|45 minutes

Nutritional Content (per serving):

Cal| 151   Fat| 12.3g   Protein| 2.1g   Carbs| 9.7g

Ingredients:

- 200 grams dried chickpeas, rinsed
- 60 grams onion, chopped roughly
- 15 grams fresh coriander
- Salt and ground black pepper, as required
- 75 milliliters olive oil, divided
- 4 garlic cloves, quartered
- 15 grams fresh parsley
- 1½ grams ground cumin
- 1¼ grams ground cinnamon

Directions:

1. In a bowl of water, soak the chickpeas and refrigerate for 24 hours.
2. Then drain the chickpeas completely.
3. Preheat your oven to 190 degrees C. Arrange a rack in the middle of oven.
4. Place 60 milliliters of oil into a large, rimmed baking sheet evenly.
5. In a food processor, add remaining oil, chickpeas, onion, garlic, herbs, cumin, cinnamon, salt and black pepper and pulse until smooth.
6. Make small equal-sized patties from the mixture.
7. Arrange the patties onto the prepared baking sheet in a single layer.
8. Bake for approximately 25-30 minutes, flipping once halfway through.
9. Serve hot.

Pasta & Pizza Recipes

Veggie Bolognese Pasta

Servings|6   Time|1 hour

Nutritional Content (per serving):

Cal| 414   Fat| 6.2g   Protein| 17.6g   Carbs| 71g

Ingredients:

- ❖ 15 milliliters olive oil
- ❖ 2 medium carrots, peeled and chopped
- ❖ 1 large courgette, chopped
- ❖ 120 milliliters dry red wine
- ❖ 1 (410-gram) can diced tomatoes with juice
- ❖ 1½ grams dried oregano
- ❖ Pinch of red pepper flakes
- ❖ 1 large onion, chopped finely
- ❖ 225 grams fresh mushrooms, chopped
- ❖ 3 garlic cloves, minced
- ❖ 1 (225-gram) can crushed tomatoes with juice
- ❖ 55 grams Parmesan cheese, grated
- ❖ 1½ grams ground black pepper
- ❖ 450 grams whole-wheat pasta

Directions:

1. In a saucepan, heat oil over medium-high heat and sauté the carrots and onion for about 4-5 minutes.
2. Add the mushrooms, courgette and garlic and cook and for about 5-6 minutes.
3. Stir in the wine and cook for about 2-5 minutes or until all the liquid is absorbed.
4. Stir in the tomatoes, cheese, oregano and spices and bring to a boil.
5. Adjust the heat to low and simmer, covered for about 25-30 minutes.
6. Meanwhile, in a large pan of salted water, cook the rigatoni until al dente or according to package's instructions.
7. Drain the rigatoni well.
8. Transfer the rigatoni onto serving plates and serve with the topping of sauce.

Tomato Pasta

Servings|4   Time|30 minutes

Nutritional Content (per serving):

Cal| 262   Fat| 9.5g   Protein| 5.2g   Carbs| 40.9g

Ingredients:

- 225 grams linguini pasta
- 1 garlic clove, minced
- 5 grams dried basil, crushed
- 5 grams dried thyme, crushed
- 30 milliliters olive oil
- 5 grams dried oregano, crushed
- 400 grams tomatoes, chopped

Directions:

1. In a pan of lightly salted boiling water, add the pasta and cook for about 8-10 minutes or according to package's directions.
2. Drain the pasta well.
3. In a large wok, heat oil over medium heat and sauté the garlic for about 1 minute.
4. Stir in herbs and sauté for about 1 minute more.
5. Add the pasta and cook for about 2-3 minutes or until heated completely.
6. Fold in tomatoes and remove from heat.
7. Serve hot.

Baked Ziti

Servings|4   Time|1¼ hours

Nutritional Content (per serving):

Cal| 372   Fat| 7.1g   Protein| 20.7g   Carbs| 55.5g

Ingredients:

- ❖ 300 grams uncooked ziti pasta
- ❖ 170 grams mozzarella, shredded and divided
- ❖ 1 large egg, lightly beaten
- ❖ 1½ grams dried oregano
- ❖ Ground black pepper, as required
- ❖ 555 grams meatless spaghetti sauce, divided
- ❖ 160 grams cottage cheese
- ❖ 10 grams dried parsley
- ❖ 1¼ grams garlic powder

Directions:

1. Preheat your oven to 190 degrees C. Grease an 8-inch square baking dish.
2. In a large pan of the salted boiling water, add the pasta and cook for about 8-10 minutes.
3. Meanwhile, in a large bowl, add 225 grams of spaghetti sauce, 110 grams of mozzarella cheese, cottage cheese, egg, dried herbs, garlic powder and black pepper and mix well.
4. Drain the pasta well and stir with the cheese mixture.
5. In the bottom of the prepared baking dish, spread 75 grams of spaghetti sauce and top with the pasta mixture, followed by the remaining sauce and mozzarella cheese.
6. Cover the baking dish and bake for approximately 45 minutes.
7. Uncover and bake for approximately 5-10 minutes more.
8. Serve hot.

Chicken Pasta

Servings|4   Time|35 minutes

Nutritional Content (per serving):

Cal| 548   Fat| 18.4g   Protein| 44.8g   Carbs| 45g

Ingredients:

- ❖ 225 grams whole-wheat pasta
- ❖ 455 grams boneless, skinless chicken breasts, cut into bite-sized pieces
- ❖ 4 garlic cloves, minced
- ❖ 30 milliliters fresh lemon juice
- ❖ 180-240 grams fresh spinach, chopped
- ❖ 30 milliliters olive oil
- ❖ Salt and ground black pepper, as required
- ❖ 120 milliliters dry white wine
- ❖ 5 grams lemon zest, grated
- ❖ 30 grams Parmesan cheese, grated

Directions:

1. In a pan of boiling water, cook the pasta for about 8-10 minutes or according to package's directions.
2. Drain the pasta and set aside.
3. Meanwhile, in a large high-sided wok, heat the oil over medium-high heat and cook the chicken pieces, salt and black pepper for about 5-7 minutes, stirring occasionally.
4. Add the garlic and cook for about 1 minute, stirring continuously.
5. Stir in the wine, lemon juice and zest and bring to a gentle simmer.
6. Remove from the heat and immediately stir in the cooked pasta and spinach.
7. Cover the pan and set aside for about 4-5 minutes or until spinach is just wilted.
8. Serve with the topping of Parmesan.

Shrimp Pasta

Servings|4   Time|25 minutes

Nutritional Content (per serving):

Cal| 53   Fat| 18.9g   Protein| 33.6g   Carbs| 50.3g

Ingredients:

- ❖ 250 grams sour cream
- ❖ 3 garlic cloves, chopped
- ❖ 1¼ grams red pepper flakes
- ❖ 1 (285-gram) packages frozen spinach, thawed
- ❖ Salt and ground black pepper, as required
- ❖ 55 grams feta cheese, crumbled
- ❖ 10 grams dried basil, crushed
- ❖ 225 grams whole-wheat pasta
- ❖ 340 grams medium shrimp, peeled and deveined

Directions:

1. In a large serving bowl, add the sour cream, feta, garlic, basil, red pepper flakes and salt and mix well.
2. Set aside until using.
3. In a large pan of the lightly salted boiling water, add the fettucine and cook for about 10 minutes or according to the package's directions.
4. After 8 minutes, stir in the spinach and shrimp and cook for about 2 minutes.
5. Drain the pasta mixture well.
6. Add the hot pasta mixture into the bowl of the sour cream mixture and gently toss to coat.
7. Serve immediately.

Veggie Pizza

Servings|4   Time|25 minutes

Nutritional Content (per serving):

Cal| 579   Fat| 42.2g   Protein| 20.4g   Carbs| 33.4g

Ingredients:

- 1 prepared pizza crust
- 250 grams pesto
- 55 grams sun-dried tomatoes
- 90 grams Kalamata olives
- 115 grams feta cheese, crumbled
- 30 grams provolone cheese, shredded
- 5-10 milliliters olive oil
- 180 grams artichoke hearts, chopped
- 150 grams green capsicum, seeded and sliced
- 55 grams mozzarella cheese, shredded
- 30 grams Asiago cheese, shredded

Directions:

1. Preheat your oven to 180 degrees C.
2. Brush pizza crust with olive oil evenly.
3. Spread pesto over the pizza crust, leaving the edges.
4. Arrange the olives, sun-dried tomatoes, artichoke hearts, capsicum over pesto and sprinkle with cheeses.
5. Place the pizza directly over the oven rack and bake for approximately 10 minutes or until cheese is melted.
6. Remove from the oven and set the pizza aside for about 5 minutes before slicing.
7. Cut into desired sized slices and serve.

Pepperoni Pizza

Servings|6   Time|28 minutes

Nutritional Content (per serving):

Cal| 169   Fat| 7.8g   Protein| 7.5g   Carbs| 17.8g

Ingredients:

- ❖ 1 prepared pizza crust
- ❖ 150 grams mozzarella cheese, shredded and divided
- ❖ 55 grams artichoke hearts, quartered
- ❖ 25 grams black olives, pitted and sliced
- ❖ 40 grams alfredo sauce
- ❖ 55 grams pepperoni, sliced
- ❖ 75 grams roasted red peppers, cut into strips
- ❖ ¼ of medium red onion, sliced

Directions:

1. Preheat your oven to 230 degrees C.
2. Arrange the pizza crust onto baking sheet.
3. Spread the alfredo sauce over the crust evenly.
4. Top the crust with 140 grams of mozzarella cheese, followed by pepperoni, red peppers, artichoke hearts, onion and olives.
5. Sprinkle the top with remaining mozzarella cheese.
6. Bake for approximately 12-28 minutes or until cheese is melted.
7. Remove from the oven and set the pizza aside for about 5 minutes before slicing.
8. Cut into desired sized slices and serve.

Shrimp Pizza

Servings|6   Time|30 minutes

Nutritional Content (per serving):

Cal| 209   Fat| 10g   Protein| 15.2g   Carbs| 14.5g

Ingredients:

- ❖ 1 prepared pizza crust
- ❖ 230 grams mozzarella cheese, shredded and divided
- ❖ 30 grams sun-dried tomatoes, chopped finely
- ❖ 95 grams prepared pesto sauce
- ❖ 225 grams cooked shrimp, peeled and deveined
- ❖ 25 grams green onions, minced
- ❖ 1¼ grams red pepper flakes

Directions:

1. Preheat your oven to 230 degrees C.
1. Arrange the pizza crust onto a baking sheet.
2. Spread the pesto sauce over crust evenly and sprinkle with half of the cheese.
3. Top with the shrimp, followed by the tomatoes, remaining cheese, green onion and red pepper flakes.
4. Bake for approximately 10 minutes.
5. Remove from the oven and set aside for about 3-5 minutes before slicing.
6. Cut into desired sized slices and serve.

Chicken Flatbread Pizza

Servings|4   Time|25 minutes

Nutritional Content (per serving):

Cal| 197   Fat| 10.8g   Protein| 14.1g   Carbs| 12.1g

Ingredients:

- ❖ 2 flatbreads
- ❖ 55 grams feta cheese, crumbled
- ❖ 85 grams water-packed artichoke hearts, drained and chopped
- ❖ 70 grams cooked chicken breast, chopped
- ❖ 115 grams part-skim mozzarella cheese, shredded
- ❖ 15 milliliters Greek vinaigrette
- ❖ 30 grams Parmesan cheese, grated
- ❖ 90 grams black olives, pitted and sliced
- ❖ 1¼ grams dried basil, crushed
- ❖ Pinch of ground black pepper

Directions:

1. Preheat your oven to 200 degrees C.
2. Arrange the flatbreads onto a large ungreased baking sheet and coat each with vinaigrette.
3. Top each bread with the feta cheese, followed by the Parmesan, veggies and chicken.
4. Sprinkle with the dried herbs and black pepper.
5. Top each bread with the mozzarella cheese evenly.
6. Bake for approximately 8-10 minutes or until cheese is melted.
7. Remove from the oven and set aside for about 1-2 minutes before slicing.
8. Cut each flatbread into 2 pieces and serve.

Courgette Pita Pizza

Servings|6   Time|20 minutes

Nutritional Content (per serving):

Cal| 277   Fat| 10.9g   Protein| 11.3g   Carbs| 38.8g

Ingredients:

- 450 grams courgette, shredded and squeezed
- 1 garlic clove, grated
- Salt and ground black pepper, as required
- 55 grams marble cheese, shredded
- 40 grams Parmesan cheese, grated
- 1½ grams dried basil, crushed
- 6 whole-wheat pita breads
- 30-45 milliliters olive oil

Directions:

1. Preheat the broiler of oven. Line 2 large baking sheets with parchment paper.
2. In a bowl, add the courgette, both cheeses, garlic, basil, salt and black pepper and mix well.
3. Arrange 3 pita breads onto each of prepared baking sheet.
4. Coat each pita bread with some oil and then top with courgette mixture.
5. Broil for about 2-3 minutes or until edges become crisp and brown.
6. Now, transfer the baking sheets onto the lowest rack of oven and broil for about 1-2 minutes or until cheese is melted.
7. With a pizza cutter, cut each pizza into 4 slices and serve.

Dessert Recipes

Pistachio Ice Cream

Servings|6   Time|30 minutes

Nutritional Content (per serving):

Cal| 567   Fat| 43.9g   Protein| 12.3g   Carbs| 39.2g

Ingredients:

- ❖ 480 milliliters whole milk
- ❖ 150 grams sugar, divided
- ❖ 2½ milliliters vanilla extract
- ❖ 60 grams whole pistachios
- ❖ 125 grams unsalted pistachios, finely ground
- ❖ 5 egg yolks
- ❖ 375 grams heavy cream

Directions:

1. In a pan, add all the milk, ground pistachios and 50 grams of the sugar and bring to a boil, stirring frequently.
2. Stir in the vanilla extract and remove from the heat.
3. In a bowl, add the remaining sugar and egg yolks and with a wire whisk, beat well.
4. With a ladle, add some hot milk, stirring continuously until well combined.
5. Add the egg yolk mixture into the pan and mix well.
6. Place the pan over medium-low heat and cook for about 7-10 minutes, stirring frequently.
7. Remove from the heat and through a strainer, strain the mixture into a bowl.
8. Refrigerate the bowl for about 2 hours.
9. Remove from the refrigerator and stir in the heavy cream and whole pistachios.
10. Transfer the mixture into an ice cream maker and process according to the manufacturer's directions.
11. Now, transfer the mixture into an airtight container and freeze for about 2 hours before serving.

Chocolate Gelato

Servings|4   Time|20 minutes

Nutritional Content (per serving):

Cal| 293   Fat| 25g   Protein| 3.3g   Carbs| 16.5g

Ingredients:

- ❖ 240 grams heavy whipping cream
- ❖ 15 grams unsweetened cocoa powder
- ❖ 50 grams powdered sugar
- ❖ 2 large egg yolks
- ❖ 2½ milliliters vanilla extract

Directions:

1. In a pan, add the heavy whipping cream and sugar over medium-high heat and bring to a boil, stirring frequently
2. Adjust the heat to low and simmer for about 1 minute.
3. Stir in the cocoa powder and cook for about 2 minutes, stirring continuously.
4. Remove from the heat and set aside to cool for about 5 minutes.
5. Meanwhile, in a bowl, add the egg yolks and vanilla extract and beat well.
6. Slowly add the cream mixture into the egg yolks mixture, beating continuously until slightly frothy.
7. Freeze for about 4-6 hours, stirring after every 1 hour.

Frozen Strawberry Yogurt

Servings|6   Time|15 minutes

Nutritional Content (per serving):

Cal| 237   Fat| 2g   Protein| 14.4g   Carbs| 40.9g

Ingredients:

- ❖ 840 grams plain Greek yogurt
- ❖ 60 milliliters fresh lemon juice
- ❖ 125 grams fresh strawberries, hulled and sliced
  - ○
- ❖ 200 grams sugar
- ❖ 10 milliliters pure vanilla extract
- ❖ Pinch of salt

Directions:

1. In a bowl, add all the ingredients except the strawberries and beat until smooth.
2. Transfer the yogurt mixture into an ice cream maker and process according to the manufacturer's directions, adding the strawberry slices in the last minute.
3. Now, transfer the mixture into an airtight container and freeze for about 3-4 hours.
4. Remove from the freezer and set aside at room temperature for about 10-15 minutes before serving.

Yogurt Parfait

Servings|6   Time|30 minutes

Nutritional Content (per serving):

Cal| 187   Fat| 3.6g   Protein| 11.2g   Carbs| 30g

Ingredients:

- ❖ 560 grams plain Greek yogurt
- ❖ 60 milliliters water
- ❖ 1½ grams lime zest, grated finely
- ❖ 25 grams almonds, toasted and chopped
- ❖ 80 grams honey
- ❖ 25 grams sugar
- ❖ 1¼ grams ground cinnamon
- ❖ 1¼ milliliters vanilla extract
- ❖ 4 plums, pitted and quartered
- ❖ 2 peaches, pitted and quartered

Directions:

1. In a bowl, add the yogurt and honey and mix until well combined. Set aside.
2. In a saucepan, mix together the remaining ingredients except the almonds over medium heat and cook for about 8-10 minutes or until fruits becomes tender, stirring occasionally.
3. Remove from the heat and set aside at room temperature to cool.
4. Divide half of the yogurt mixture into 4 tall serving glasses evenly.
5. Divide the fruit mixture over yogurt evenly and top each with the remaining yogurt.
6. Garnish with almonds and serve.

Fig Cake

Servings|8   Time|1 hour 5 minutes

Nutritional Content (per serving):

Cal| 361   Fat| 15.2g   Protein| 5.7g   Carbs| 54.7g

Ingredients:

- ❖ 190 grams unbleached all-purpose flour
- ❖ 5 grams lemon zest, grated finely
- ❖ 80 grams sugar
- ❖ 90 milliliters milk
- ❖ 60 grams butter, melted
- ❖ 15 grams powdered sugar

- ❖ 3 grams baking powder
- ❖ Pinch of salt
- ❖ 5 grams lemon zest, grated finely
- ❖ 2 large eggs
- ❖ 60 milliliters extra-virgin olive oil
- ❖ 2½ milliliters vanilla extract
- ❖ 285 grams fresh figs, chopped

Directions:

1. Preheat your oven to 180 degrees C. Arrange a rack in the center portion of the oven. Grease and then lightly flour a 9-inch springform pan.
2. In a large bowl, sift together the flour, baking powder and salt.
3. Add the lemon zest and mix well.
4. In another bowl, add the sugar and eggs and beat until thick and pale yellow.
5. Add the milk, oil, butter and vanilla extract and beat until well combined.
6. Add the flour mixture and mix until well combined. Set aside for about 10 minutes.
7. In the bowl of flour mixture, add about ¾ of the figs and gently stir to combine.
8. Place the mixture into the prepared pan evenly and bake for approximately 15 minutes.
9. Remove from the oven and top the cake with the remaining figs evenly.
10. Bake for approximately 35-40 minutes or until top becomes golden brown.
11. Remove from the oven and place the pan onto a wire rack for about 10 minutes.
12. Remove the cake from pan and place onto the wire rack to cool completely.
13. Dust with the powdered sugar and cut into desired sized slices before serving.

Chocolate Mousse

Servings|4   Time|40 minutes

Nutritional Content (per serving):

Cal| 277   Fat| 10.8g   Protein| 17.6g   Carbs| 26.7g

Ingredients:

- ❖ 100 grams dark chocolate, chopped
- ❖ 2½ milliliters vanilla extract
- ❖ 180 milliliters milk
- ❖ 20 grams honey
- ❖ 560 grams plain Greek yogurt

Directions:

1. In a pan, add the chocolate and milk over medium-low heat and cook for about 3-5 minutes or until chocolate melts, stirring continuously.
2. Add the honey and vanilla extract and stir to combine well.
3. Remove from the heat and set aside at room temperature to cool slightly.
4. In a large glass bowl, place the yogurt and chocolate mixture and gently stir to combine.
5. Refrigerate to chill for about 2 hours.
6. Serve with the topping of the raspberries and chocolate shaving.

Quinoa Brownies

Servings|16   Time|19 minutes

Nutritional Content (per serving):

Cal| 202   Fat| 8.8g   Protein| 3.9g   Carbs| 26.9g

Ingredients:

- 190 grams dry quinoa, rinsed
- 4 (115-gram) semi-sweet chocolate bars, chopped
- 2½ milliliters vanilla extract
- 15 grams natural peanut butter

Directions:

1. Heat a large, heavy-bottomed pan over medium-high heat.
2. Add the quinoa in 4 batches, 50 grams at a time and for about 1 minute, swirling the pan continuously.
3. Transfer each batch of quinoa into a bowl.
4. Meanwhile, in a microwave-safe bowl, add the chocolate and microwave on High until melted, stirring after every 30 seconds.
5. In the bowl of quinoa, add the melted chocolate, peanut butter and vanilla extract and mix until well combined.
6. Place the mixture into a parchment paper-lined baking sheet evenly and with the back of a spoon, spread into ½-inch thickness.
7. Refrigerate until set completely.
8. Cut into desired sized squares and serve.

Baklava

Servings|18   Time|1 hour10 minutes

Nutritional Content (per serving):

Cal| 506   Fat| 28.2g   Protein| 8.6g   Carbs| 58g

Ingredients:

- ❖ 455 grams mixed nuts (pistachios, almonds, walnuts), chopped
- ❖ 225 grams butter, melted
- ❖ 240 milliliters water
- ❖ 5 milliliters vanilla extract
- ❖ 5 grams ground cinnamon
- ❖ 1 (1150-gram) package phyllo dough
- ❖ 200 grams sugar
- ❖ 160 grams honey

Directions:

1. Preheat your oven to 180 degrees C. Grease a 9x13-inch baking dish.
2. In a bowl, add the nuts and cinnamon and toss to coat well. Set aside.
3. Unroll the phyllo dough and cut in half.
4. Arrange 2 dcugh sheets into the prepared baking dish and coat with some butter.
5. Repeat with 8 dough sheets in layers and sprinkle with 15-20 grams of nut mixture.
6. Repeat with remaining dough sheets, butter and nuts.
7. With a sharp knife, cut into diamond shapes all the way to the bottom of the baking dish.
8. Bake for approximately 50 minutes or until top becomes golden and crisp.
9. Meanwhile, for sauce: in a pan, add the sugar and water and cook until sugar is melted, stirring continuously.
10. Stir in the honey and vanilla extract and simmer for about 20 minutes.
11. Remove the baklava from oven and immediately place the sauce on top evenly.
12. Set aside to cool before serving.

Tiramisu

Servings|9   Time|15 minutes

Nutritional Content (per serving):

Cal| 227   Fat| 8.8g   Protein| 8.4g   Carbs| 26.8g

Ingredients:

- ❖ 120 grams heavy whipping cream
- ❖ 240 milliliters fat-free milk
- ❖ 24 crisp ladyfinger cookies
- ❖ 560 grams vanilla yogurt
- ❖ 120 milliliters brewed espresso, cooled
- ❖ Cocoa powder, for dusting

Directions:

1. In a small bowl, add cream and beat until stiff peaks form.
2. Gently, fold in the yogurt.
3. In the bottom of an 8-inch square dish, place 150 grams of cream mixture evenly.
4. In a shallow dish, mix together the milk and espresso.
5. Dip 12 ladyfinger cookies into espresso mixture, allowing excess to drip off.
6. Arrange the dipped ladyfinger cookies over cream mixture in a single layer.
7. Top with half of the remaining cream mixture evenly and dust with cocoa powder.
8. Repeat the layers.
9. Cover the baking dish and refrigerate for at least 2 hours before serving.

Roasted Pears

Servings|6   Time|35 minutes

Nutritional Content (per serving):

Cal| 207   Fat| 9.5g   Protein| 3.2g   Carbs| 30.8g

Ingredients:

- ❖ 80 grams pear nectar
- ❖ 30 grams butter, melted
- ❖ 3 ripe medium Bosc pears, peeled and cored
- ❖ 40 grams walnuts, chopped
- ❖ 60 grams honey
- ❖ 5 grams orange zest, grated
- ❖ 60 grams mascarpone cheese
- ❖ 20 grams powdered sugar

Directions:

1. Preheat your oven to 200 degrees C.
2. In a bowl, add the pear nectar, honey, butter and orange zest and mix well.
3. In a 2-quart rectangular baking dish, arrange the pears, cut sides down and top with the honey mixture.
4. Roast for about 20-25 minutes, spooning liquid over pears occasionally.
5. Remove from the oven and transfer the pears onto serving plates with some of the cooking liquid.
6. In a bowl, add the mascarpone cheese and powdered sugar and mix well.
7. Top the pears with the cheese mixture and serve with the garnishing of walnuts.

Thank you for going through the book, I sincerely hope you enjoyed the recipes.

As I said before, a lot of time went into creating so many recipes and I really hope you're satisfied with the recipes provided.

I'm trying really hard to create the best recipes I can and I'm always open to feedback so whether you liked or disliked the book feel free to write on my email at deliciousrecipes.publishing@gmail.com. I always reply and love to communicate with everybody. If you didn't like the recipes you can reach out and I'll share another cookbook or two for free in order to try to improve your experience at least a little bit.

Thank you for going through the recipes, enjoy!

Index

E

egg, 19, 20, 32, 37, 78, 97, 106, 107
espresso, 114

F

farro, 81
fennel bulbs, 20
fennel seeds, 23
feta cheese, 21, 33, 37, 40, 45, 61, 66, 71, 81, 84, 85, 90, 99, 100, 103
figs, 12, 15, 24, 110
flatbreads, 103
fresh basil, 30, 31, 45, 55, 60, 67, 68, 72, 74, 76, 84
fresh coriander, 77, 87, 93
fresh dill, 27, 37, 55, 56, 57, 90
fresh parsley, 21, 25, 29, 32, 37, 42, 52, 53, 61, 64, 65, 66, 69, 73, 76, 79, 80, 81, 82, 93

G

garlic, 21, 23, 25, 28, 29, 30, 31, 32, 33, 35, 36, 37, 39, 41, 42, 43, 44, 46, 47, 48, 49, 50, 51, 52, 53, 55, 56, 57, 60, 61, 62, 64, 65, 66, 67, 68, 69, 72, 73, 76, 78, 79, 80, 81, 82, 84, 85, 86, 88, 89, 90, 92, 93, 95, 96, 97, 98, 99, 104
garlic croutons, 84
garlic powder, 29, 32, 36, 41, 48, 57, 73, 88, 97
garlic salt, 56
garlic sausage, 79
goat cheese, 20
Gorgonzola cheese, 41
Great Northern beans, 79
Greek seasoning, 63, 76
Greek vinaigrette, 103
Greek yogurt, 7, 8, 12, 17, 55, 57, 73, 90, 108, 109, 111
green onion, 76, 82, 102
green peas, 34
ground allspice, 49, 52, 79
ground cinnamon, 8, 15, 16, 17, 93, 109, 113
ground coriander, 52, 55, 62, 75
ground ginger, 77
ground turkey, 36, 37, 78
ground turmeric, 27, 62, 69, 73

H

half-and-half, 58
halibut, 63
heavy cream, 29, 41, 106
heavy whipping cream, 47, 107, 114
honey, 8, 9, 11, 12, 14, 17, 45, 67, 68, 71, 109, 111, 113, 115

I

ice cubes, 7, 8, 9
Italian seasoning, 30, 91

J

jalapeño pepper, 62

K

kale, 73, 78, 81
kelp powder, 73

L

ladyfinger cookies, 114
lamb loin chops, 50
lamb shanks, 51
leg of lamb, 52, 53
lemon, 10, 23, 25, 26, 27, 28, 33, 34, 35, 39, 40, 41, 46, 49, 50, 52, 55, 56, 58, 60, 61, 63, 64, 65, 69, 76, 80, 81, 86, 89, 92, 98, 108, 110
lemon pepper seasoning, 41, 58
lentils, 77, 90
lettuce, 74
lime, 57, 62, 71, 74, 109
linguini pasta, 96

M

mango, 8
maple syrup, 13, 16, 18
marble cheese, 104
marinara sauce, 32, 91
Medjool dates, 7
milk, 11, 13, 15, 17, 37, 106, 110, 111, 114
mint, 10, 49, 71
mixed berries, 14
molasses, 16
mozzarella cheese, 32, 72, 88, 97, 100, 101, 102, 103
mushrooms, 29, 31, 35, 47, 77, 95
mussels, 68, 69

N

nutmeg, 49

O

oats, 9, 13, 18, 19

Printed in Great Britain
by Amazon